Practice, Practice, Practice!

MULTIPLICATION & DIVISION

by Christine Hood

New York • Toronto • London • Auckland • Sydney
Mexico City • New Delhi • Hong Kong • Buenos Aires

Teaching
Resources

Cover design by Maria Lilja

Cover and interior illustrations by Teresa Anderko

Interior design by Ellen Matlach for Boultinghouse & Boultinghouse, Inc.

ISBN: 0-439-59728-5

Contents

Multiplication

Division

Introduction

Welcome to *Practice, Practice, Practice! Multiplication & Division*. This book is packed with more than 50 reproducible activity sheets that give students practice in multiplication and division facts up to 12. The practice pages are flexible and easy to use—kids can complete them at home or in school, independently or in groups. Each activity features appealing illustrations, topics kids enjoy, and simple instructions so that students can work on their own. Pull out these practice pages for quick activities during the school day, or send them home as skill-building homework assignments.

The activities in *Practice, Practice, Practice! Multiplication & Division* also coordinate with the standards recommended by the National Council of Teachers of Mathematics (NCTM). Some of the NCTM standards for content and processes covered in this book include numbers and operations, patterns, functions, geometry and spatial sense, data analysis, problem solving, reasoning and proof, communication, and representation.

These pages were designed to appeal to third and fourth graders. The topics relate to their world and interests: school, sports, pets, favorite foods, friends, shopping, and more! In addition, students will enjoy the variety of formats. They'll put together a picture puzzle, use a color key to color a scene, play coin-toss games, crack secret codes, and much, much more. Many of the practice pages challenge students to go beyond solving multiplication and division problems. For instance, in some of the activities, students will need to use their answers to complete word finds, solve crossword puzzles, and answer riddles. As further reinforcement, terms such as *equation*, *product*, and *quotient* are used throughout the book to help students become accustomed to reading and using the related math language.

For your convenience, a comprehensive answer key is included at the end of the book (pages 61–64). Each practice page is listed by title and page number. This easy reference will allow you or your students to check their completed pages for correct answers.

Whether you use the pages from *Practice, Practice, Practice! Multiplication & Division* for homework or class work, they are sure to give your students an enjoyable way to get the extra practice and reinforcement they need to succeed in math!

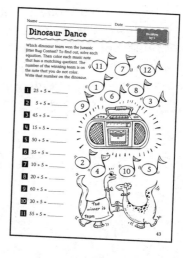

How to Use This Book

These practice pages were designed for flexible use. Students can work on them individually, in pairs, in small groups, or as a whole class. In addition, the ready-to-use pages provide ideal activities to leave for substitute teachers to use with the class. Have students work on the sheets:

- for reinforcement of basic multiplication and division facts

- for review after a math unit is completed

- when they are finished with other class work

- as an activity to start or finish the day

- after lunch to settle back into learning

- as math center activities for practicing multiplication and division facts

- as skill-building homework activities

Refer to the table of contents to locate the practice pages that address a particular fact for multiplication or division. For easy reference, the specific facts are also listed in a box near the top of each practice page. You can use the pages in the order they are presented or rearrange them to suit the needs of your students.

Most of the practice pages require only a pencil and eraser. A few require scissors, glue, and crayons. If you are sending home the sheets as homework, review the directions in advance to answer any questions that students have about the activities. You might also review the materials and modify them if necessary.

When students work on the practice pages independently, encourage them to read the directions and problems carefully before they begin to write on their pages. If desired, you may set up a buddy system, so that students can seek assistance from other classmates if the need arises.

If you plan to use the practice pages in a math center, place all the materials needed to complete the activities in the center. You may want to make a special folder for the activity pages for each multiplication and division fact family. Include a list of student names and a copy of the answer key for those pages in the folder, too. Then when students visit the center, they can work the assigned practice page, use the answer key to check their work, and check their names off the list to show that they finished the page.

Feel free to modify any of the practice pages to fit your students' specific needs. For example, you might replace the "× 2" on page 9 (*Target Practice*) with any number, from 1 to 12, to create a practice page for a different fact family. Encourage students to work together and share their problem-solving strategies as they work their way through the practice pages in this book.

Name _____ Date _____

Picture Puzzler

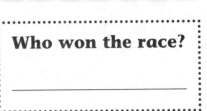

Solve each problem. Then cut out the boxes. To make a picture, put the boxes back together in the order of their products, from 1 to 12. Glue the picture onto another sheet of paper. Then answer the question.

Who won the race?

_____

4 × 1

1 × 3

1 × 11

1 × 5

10 × 1

8 × 1

2 × 1

1 × 9 Finish!

1 × 1 Start

12 × 1

6 × 1

1 × 7

Name _____ Date _____

Write the Equation

Write an equation to show how to multiply the
items in each picture by 1. Then write the product.
The first problem has been done for you.

1 how many apples
in the basket

$$7 \times 1 = 7$$

2 how many wings
on the bird

_____

3 how many petals
on the flower

_____

4 how many legs
on the spider

_____

5 how many spots
on the ladybug

_____

6 how many stars
on the flag

_____

7 how many
cupcakes on
the tray

_____

8 how many hearts
on the card

_____

Practice, Practice, Practice! Multiplication & Division Scholastic Teaching Resources

Target Practice

Multiply each number in the target by 2. On the back of the page, write the equation and find the product. Show how you got your answer. Then write the product in the space on the target.

Mountain Climber

Help Benny Bear climb up to the honey.
To show him the right path, color all the
spaces that have numbers that are multiples
of 2. Then use the numbers in the path
to solve the problems on the tree.

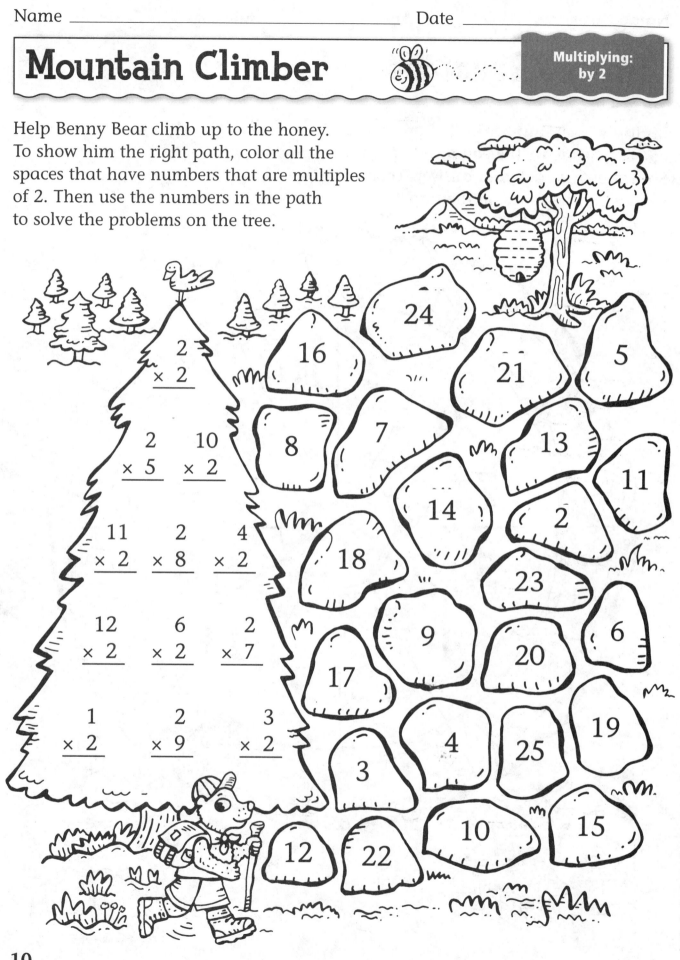

On the tree:

$$2 \times 2$$

$$\begin{array}{cc} 2 & 10 \\ \times 5 & \times 2 \end{array}$$

$$\begin{array}{ccc} 11 & 2 & 4 \\ \times 2 & \times 8 & \times 2 \end{array}$$

$$\begin{array}{ccc} 12 & 6 & 2 \\ \times 2 & \times 2 & \times 7 \end{array}$$

$$\begin{array}{ccc} 1 & 2 & 3 \\ \times 2 & \times 9 & \times 2 \end{array}$$

Numbers on rocks: 24, 16, 21, 5, 8, 7, 13, 11, 14, 2, 18, 23, 6, 9, 20, 17, 4, 25, 19, 3, 10, 15, 12, 22

Practice, Practice, Practice! Multiplication & Division   Scholastic Teaching Resources

Kitty Riddle

Use a yellow crayon to color all the lemons that have numbers that are multiples of 3. To solve the riddle, write the yellow letters on the lines in the order that they appear on the lemons. Then use the yellow numbers to solve the problems below.

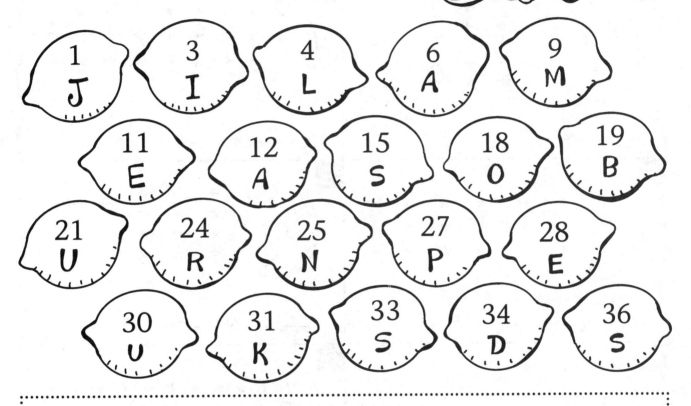

| 1 J | 3 I | 4 L | 6 A | 9 M |

| 11 E | 12 A | 15 S | 18 O | 19 B |

| 21 U | 24 R | 25 N | 27 P | 28 E |

| 30 U | 31 K | 33 S | 34 D | 36 S |

Riddle: What did the cat say when she ate the lemon?

Answer: ___ ___ ___ ___ ___ ___ ___ ___ ___ ___ ___!

$$\begin{array}{r} 11 \\ \times\ 3 \\ \hline \end{array} \qquad \begin{array}{r} 3 \\ \times\ 1 \\ \hline \end{array} \qquad \begin{array}{r} 3 \\ \times\ 3 \\ \hline \end{array} \qquad \begin{array}{r} 7 \\ \times\ 3 \\ \hline \end{array} \qquad \begin{array}{r} 4 \\ \times\ 3 \\ \hline \end{array} \qquad \begin{array}{r} 3 \\ \times\ 5 \\ \hline \end{array}$$

$$\begin{array}{r} 12 \\ \times\ 3 \\ \hline \end{array} \qquad \begin{array}{r} 6 \\ \times\ 3 \\ \hline \end{array} \qquad \begin{array}{r} 3 \\ \times\ 9 \\ \hline \end{array} \qquad \begin{array}{r} 2 \\ \times\ 3 \\ \hline \end{array} \qquad \begin{array}{r} 10 \\ \times\ 3 \\ \hline \end{array} \qquad \begin{array}{r} 8 \\ \times\ 3 \\ \hline \end{array}$$

Practice, Practice, Practice! Multiplication & Division   Scholastic Teaching Resources

11

Starry Nights

Circle each row of stars in the pictures. Write an equation that shows how to multiply the stars in each night sky. Then write the product. The first problem has been done for you.

1

$$\underline{5} \times \underline{3} = \underline{15}$$

2

$$\underline{} \times \underline{} = \underline{}$$

3

$$\underline{} \times \underline{} = \underline{}$$

4

$$\underline{} \times \underline{} = \underline{}$$

5

$$\underline{} \times \underline{} = \underline{}$$

6

$$\underline{} \times \underline{} = \underline{}$$

7

$$\underline{} \times \underline{} = \underline{}$$

8

$$\underline{} \times \underline{} = \underline{}$$

Practice, Practice, Practice! Multiplication & Division   Scholastic Teaching Resources

Runaway Riddle

Write the product for each equation. On the back of the page, show how you got your answers. To solve the riddle, find the box that has the product that matches the number below each line. Then write the letter from that box on the line. The first one has been done for you.

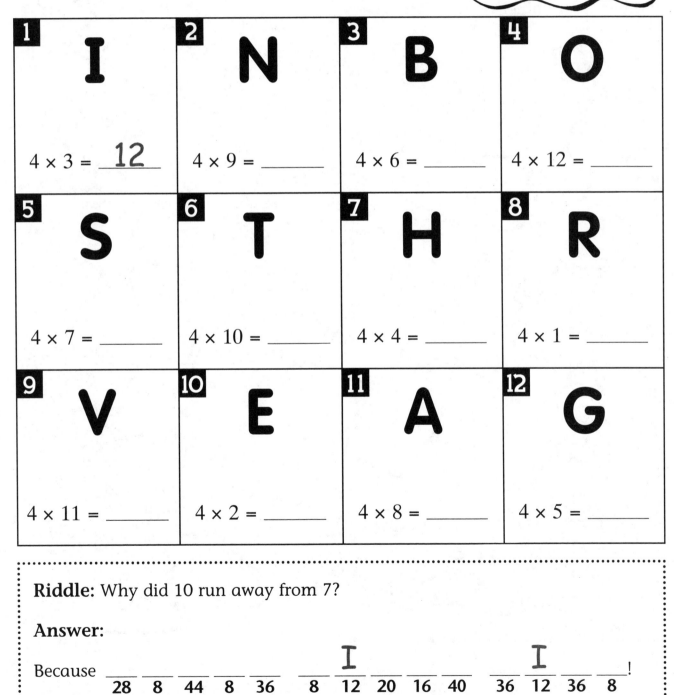

1 I $4 \times 3 = \underline{12}$	**2** N $4 \times 9 = \underline{}$	**3** B $4 \times 6 = \underline{}$	**4** O $4 \times 12 = \underline{}$
5 S $4 \times 7 = \underline{}$	**6** T $4 \times 10 = \underline{}$	**7** H $4 \times 4 = \underline{}$	**8** R $4 \times 1 = \underline{}$
9 V $4 \times 11 = \underline{}$	**10** E $4 \times 2 = \underline{}$	**11** A $4 \times 8 = \underline{}$	**12** G $4 \times 5 = \underline{}$

Riddle: Why did 10 run away from 7?

Answer:

Because __ __ __ __ __ __ I __ __ __ __ __ I __ __ !
           28 8 44 8 36   8 12 20 16 40   36 12 36 8

Crossing Paths

Help each animal complete the number pattern on the path to its tree. On path A, fill in the missing numbers that are multiples of 4. On path B, fill in the missing numbers that are multiples of 5. Color each path a different color. The paths cross at two numbers that are multiples of 4 and 5. Write these numbers on the lines.

_____ and _____ are multiples of 4 and 5.

Practice, Practice, Practice! Multiplication & Division Scholastic Teaching Resources

Number Tower

Solve each problem. Find the number word in the key for each product. Then write the word on the tower. Hint: For number words with hyphens, do not write the hyphen (-).

To discover the mystery product, read the number word that appears in the shaded spaces on the tower. Write that number on the line below. Then write an equation for the product.

KEY		
fifteen	forty	ten
fifty	forty-five	thirty
five	sixty	twenty

1 5 × 8 = _____

2 12 × 5 = _____

3 3 × 5 = _____

4 5 × 2 = _____

5 5 × 9 = _____

6 10 × 5 = _____

7 5 × 6 = _____

8 1 × 5 = _____

9 5 × 4 = _____

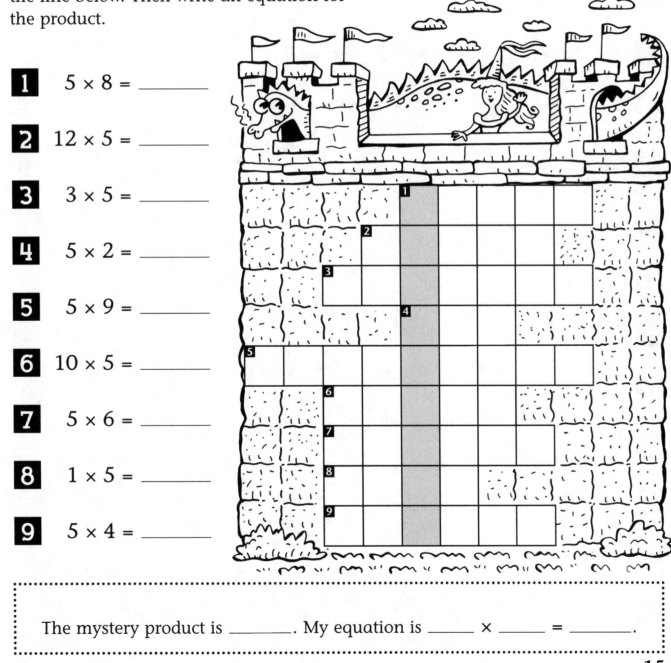

The mystery product is _____. My equation is _____ × _____ = _____.

Lucky Number

To help Sandy Squirrel find the lucky number, solve each problem. Find the product on a leaf. Then color the leaf green. The lucky number is on the leaf that you do not color. Write that number on Sandy's sign.

1 $5 \times 5 =$ _____

2 $5 \times 12 =$ _____

3 $9 \times 5 =$ _____

4 $5 \times 1 =$ _____

5 $7 \times 5 =$ _____

6 $5 \times 11 =$ _____

7 $5 \times 3 =$ _____

8 $4 \times 5 =$ _____

9 $10 \times 5 =$ _____

10 $5 \times 0 =$ _____

11 $5 \times 6 =$ _____

12 $8 \times 5 =$ _____

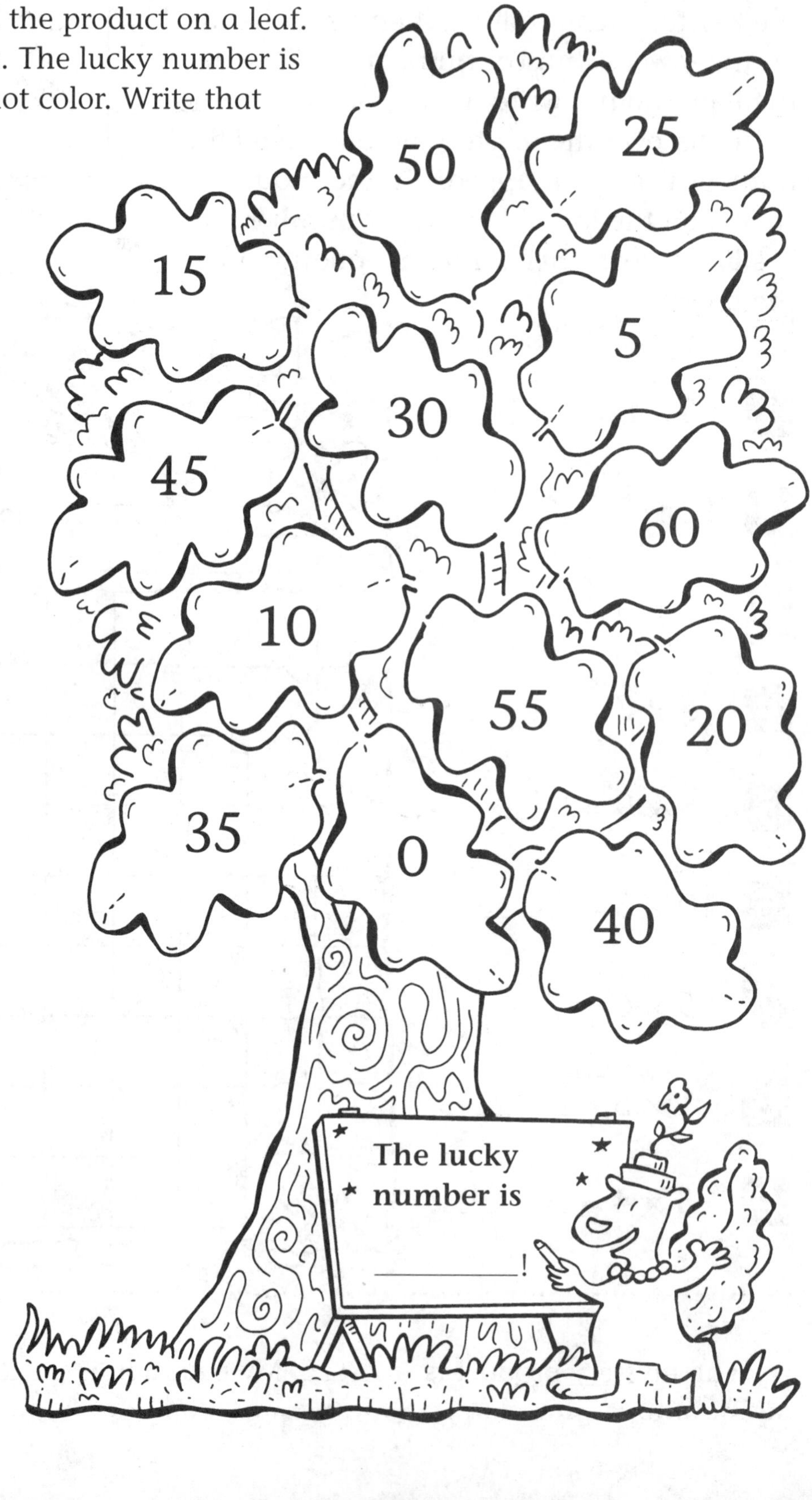

50   25   15   5   30   45   60   10   55   20   35   0   40

The lucky number is _____ !

Practice, Practice, Practice! Multiplication & Division   Scholastic Teaching Resources

Secret Code

Look at the secret symbol in each problem. Check the key to find the symbol and its matching number. Write that number in the equation. Then solve the equation. Use the back of the page to show how you got your answers.

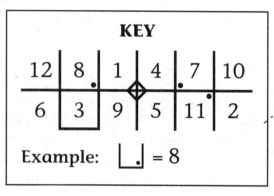

KEY

12	8	1	4	7	10
6	3	9	5	11	2

Example: ⌐• = 8

1

6 × ⌐

6 × _____ = _____

2

6 × ⌐•

6 × _____ = _____

3

6 × ∟•

6 × _____ = _____

4

6 × Γ

6 × _____ = _____

5

6 × ⌐|

6 × _____ = _____

6

6 × □

6 × _____ = _____

7

6 × ⌐

6 × _____ = _____

8

6 × ∟

6 × _____ = _____

9

6 × ∟⌐

6 × _____ = _____

10

6 × ⌐|

6 × _____ = _____

11

6 × ∪

6 × _____ = _____

12

6 × •∪

6 × _____ = _____

Hit the Trail!

Read each word problem. Then use the information on the sign to write and solve an equation for the problem.

Crystal Canyon Hiking Trails

All trails are 6 miles!

Black Bear Trail   Red Rabbit Trail
Early Eagle Trail   Wild Wind Trail
Misty Meadow Trail   Friendly Fawn Trail

1 Mike hiked Black Bear Trail four times. How many miles did he hike?

_____ × _____ miles = _____ miles

2 Chelsea and her sister hiked Friendly Fawn Trail three times. How many miles did they hike?

_____ × _____ miles = _____ miles

3 Devon and Shania hiked Early Eagle Trail seven times. How many miles did they hike?

_____ × _____ miles = _____ miles

4 Aliya hiked Red Rabbit Trail nine times. How many miles did he hike?

_____ × _____ miles = _____ miles

5 Wyatt and Tanya hiked Misty Meadow Trail and Wild Wind Trail. How many miles did they hike?

_____ × _____ miles = _____ miles

6 Carlos and his dad hiked each trail once. How many miles did they hike?

_____ × _____ miles = _____ miles

Practice, Practice, Practice! Multiplication & Division   Scholastic Teaching Resources

Name _____ Date _____

Diamond Challenge

Cut out the diamonds. Then match each problem to its product. Put the matching sides of the diamonds together. When finished, you will have one large shape. Hint: The star belongs at the top of the large shape.

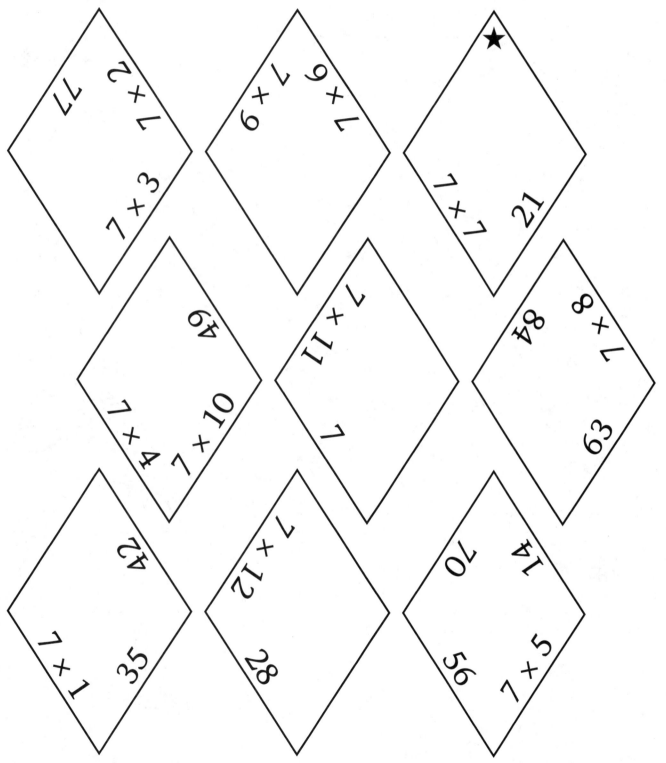

Practice, Practice, Practice! Multiplication & Division   Scholastic Teaching Resources

19

Name _____ Date _____

Sunny Sevens

Help the sun find its way through the clouds.
To mark the path, circle all the numbers that
are multiples of 7. Then use the numbers in
the path to solve the problems.

8	7	12	7	7	5
× 7	× 2	× 7	× 1	× 3	× 7

11	7	9	10	7	6
× 7	× 7	× 7	× 7	× 4	× 7

Practice, Practice, Practice! Multiplication & Division Scholastic Teaching Resources

Presto Products!

To help Rabbit find the magic number, solve each equation. Find that product on a star. Then color the star red. The magic number is on the star that you do not color. Write that number on Rabbit's cape.

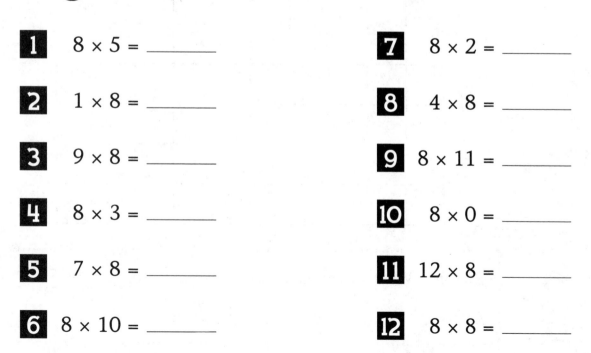

The magic number is _____!

1 $8 \times 5 =$ _____

2 $1 \times 8 =$ _____

3 $9 \times 8 =$ _____

4 $8 \times 3 =$ _____

5 $7 \times 8 =$ _____

6 $8 \times 10 =$ _____

7 $8 \times 2 =$ _____

8 $4 \times 8 =$ _____

9 $8 \times 11 =$ _____

10 $8 \times 0 =$ _____

11 $12 \times 8 =$ _____

12 $8 \times 8 =$ _____

Easy Eights

Solve each problem. Find the number word in the key for each product. Then write the word in the puzzle. Hint: For number words with hyphens, do not write the hyphen (-).

To solve the rhyming riddle, unscramble the letters in the gray puzzle boxes.

Key

zero	forty-eight
eight	fifty-six
sixteen	sixty-four
twenty-four	seventy-two
forty	eighty-eight

Across

1. $8 \times 3 =$ _____

3. $8 \times 0 =$ _____

6. $8 \times 8 =$ _____

7. $8 \times 2 =$ _____

9. $8 \times 11 =$ _____

10. $8 \times 9 =$ _____

Down

2. $8 \times 6 =$ _____

4. $8 \times 7 =$ _____

5. $8 \times 5 =$ _____

8. $8 \times 1 =$ _____

Riddle: What do you call a sea animal's dream?

Answer: A ___ ___ ___ ___ ___ ___ ___ ___ ___ ___ !

Practice, Practice, Practice! Multiplication & Division Scholastic Teaching Resources

Nine-Square Dare

Who is the winner of Nine-Square Dare? To find out, solve the problems. Then draw an X on all the matching products that you find on each player's card. The player with more Xs wins! Write that player's name on the line below.

Nine-Square Dare

16	90	21
63	27	38
36	40	72

Name _Riley_

Nine-Square Dare

9	81	29
18	72	54
45	99	84

Name _Tina_

$$\begin{array}{c} 8 \\ \times\ 9 \\ \hline \end{array} \qquad \begin{array}{c} 9 \\ \times\ 2 \\ \hline \end{array} \qquad \begin{array}{c} 11 \\ \times\ 9 \\ \hline \end{array} \qquad \begin{array}{c} 10 \\ \times\ 9 \\ \hline \end{array} \qquad \begin{array}{c} 9 \\ \times\ 1 \\ \hline \end{array} \qquad \begin{array}{c} 7 \\ \times\ 9 \\ \hline \end{array}$$

$$\begin{array}{c} 12 \\ \times\ 9 \\ \hline \end{array} \qquad \begin{array}{c} 9 \\ \times\ 4 \\ \hline \end{array} \qquad \begin{array}{c} 9 \\ \times\ 9 \\ \hline \end{array} \qquad \begin{array}{c} 6 \\ \times\ 9 \\ \hline \end{array} \qquad \begin{array}{c} 3 \\ \times\ 9 \\ \hline \end{array} \qquad \begin{array}{c} 9 \\ \times\ 5 \\ \hline \end{array}$$

The winner of Nine-Square Dare is _____.

Practice, Practice, Practice! Multiplication & Division   Scholastic Teaching Resources

23

Name _____ Date _____

Prehistoric Pun

Solve each equation. Then use a green crayon to color
the leaf over the correct product. To solve the riddle,
write the green letters on the lines in the order that
they appear on the leaves.

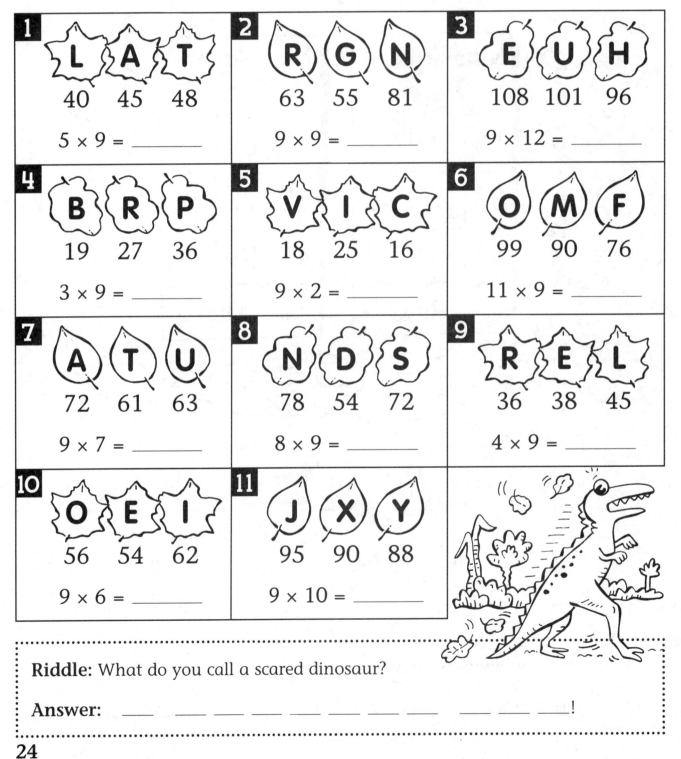

1

L A T
40 45 48

$5 \times 9 =$ _____

2

R G N
63 55 81

$9 \times 9 =$ _____

3

E U H
108 101 96

$9 \times 12 =$ _____

4

B R P
19 27 36

$3 \times 9 =$ _____

5

V I C
18 25 16

$9 \times 2 =$ _____

6

O M F
99 90 76

$11 \times 9 =$ _____

7

A T U
72 61 63

$9 \times 7 =$ _____

8

N D S
78 54 72

$8 \times 9 =$ _____

9

R E L
36 38 45

$4 \times 9 =$ _____

10

O E I
56 54 62

$9 \times 6 =$ _____

11

J X Y
95 90 88

$9 \times 10 =$ _____

Riddle: What do you call a scared dinosaur?

Answer: ____ ____ ____ ____ ____ ____ ____ ____ ____ ____ ____ ____!

24

Lasso Match

Leo Lizard just learned that the numbers in a multiplication problem can be put in any order without changing the product. This is called the **commutative property** of multiplication.

To help Leo lasso each pair of problems that shares the same product, solve each problem on the left. Write the product in the loop. Then draw a line from the loop to the problem on the right that has the same product. The first problem has been done for you.

1 7×10 $=$ _70_ $=$

2 10×3 $=$ _____ $=$

3 10×4 $=$ _____ $=$

4 2×10 $=$ _____ $=$

5 10×8 $=$ _____ $=$

6 5×10 $=$ _____ $=$

7 6×10 $=$ _____ $=$

8 10×9 $=$ _____ $=$

A. 8×10

B. 4×10

C. 10×5

D. 9×10

E. 10×7

F. 3×10

G. 10×2

H. 10×6

Snack Shop

The value of a dime is 10¢. Write the correct number in each equation to show how many dimes are needed to buy each item. Then find the product. On the back of the page, show two ways that you can find each product.

1 Chips
_____ × 10¢ = _____ ¢

2 (ice cream cone)
_____ × 10¢ = _____ ¢

3 (balloon)
_____ × 10¢ = _____ ¢

4 Soda
_____ × 10¢ = _____ ¢

5 Crazy Bubble Gum
_____ × 10¢ = _____ ¢

6 Triple Delight Chocolate Bar
_____ × 10¢ = _____ ¢

7 Popcorn
_____ × 10¢ = _____ ¢

8 (hot dog)
_____ × 10¢ = _____ ¢

9 Toasty!
_____ × 10¢ = _____ ¢

Practice, Practice, Practice! Multiplication & Division Scholastic Teaching Resources

Teddy Tale

Solve each equation. On the back of the page, show how you got your answers. To solve the riddle, find the problem that has the product that matches the number below each line. Then write the letter from that box on the line.

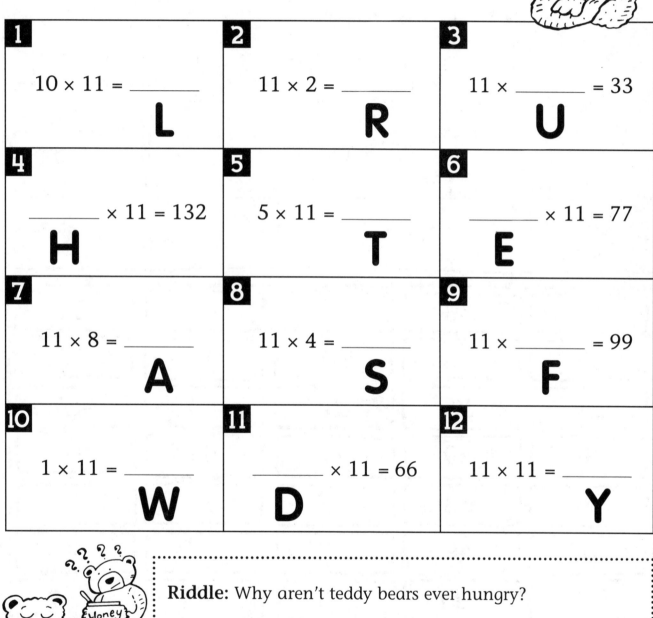

1

$10 \times 11 =$ _____

L

2

$11 \times 2 =$ _____

R

3

$11 \times$ _____ $= 33$

U

4

_____ $\times 11 = 132$

H

5

$5 \times 11 =$ _____

T

6

_____ $\times 11 = 77$

E

7

$11 \times 8 =$ _____

A

8

$11 \times 4 =$ _____

S

9

$11 \times$ _____ $= 99$

F

10

$1 \times 11 =$ _____

W

11

_____ $\times 11 = 66$

D

12

$11 \times 11 =$ _____

Y

Riddle: Why aren't teddy bears ever hungry?

Answer: Because they ___ ___ ___
$\qquad$ 88 22 7

___ ___ ___ ___ ___ ___ ___ ___ ___ ___ ___ ___ ___
88 110 11 88 121 44   44 55 3 9 9 7 6

Walk the Wall

It's time for Cool Jack Cat to take his midnight walk along the top of the wall. To help him find the climbing path up the wall, solve each equation. Then find and color each brick that has a matching product. On the back of the page, show two ways that you can find each product.

$$\begin{array}{ccccc} 7 & 11 & 8 & 11 & 11 & 10 \\ \times 11 & \times 2 & \times 11 & \times 1 & \times 11 & \times 11 \end{array}$$

$$\begin{array}{ccccc} 11 & 12 & 4 & 11 & 9 & 11 \\ \times 3 & \times 11 & \times 11 & \times 6 & \times 11 & \times 5 \end{array}$$

15	33	27	60	84
59	88	65	12	72
21	55	22	64	47
48	39	77	99	101
96	63	32	11	76
108	49	121	110	30
20	111	66	92	124
36	94	44	132	56

Magic Multiplication

Multiply the numbers in the squares across and then down. Write the products.

To check your answers, add the two products across. Write the sum in the corner square. Then add the two products down. If this sum matches the number in the corner, your answers are correct. The answers in the first box have been done for you.

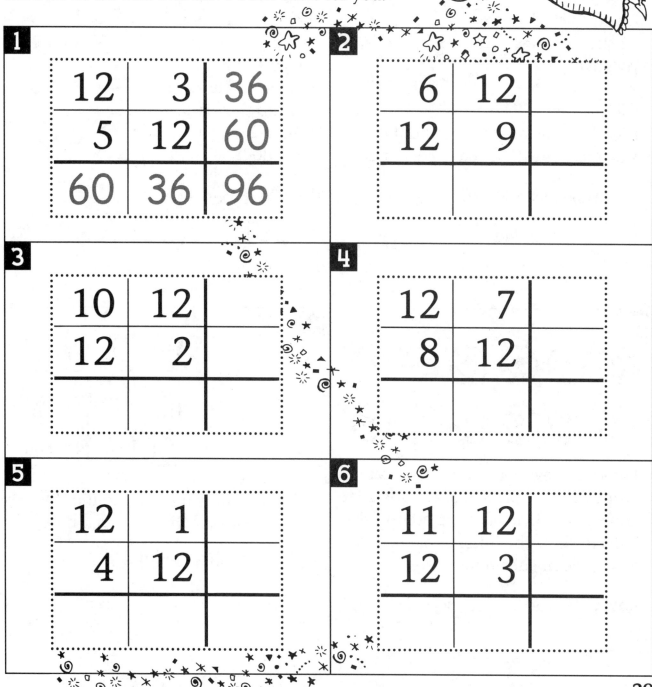

1

12	3	36
5	12	60
60	36	96

2

6	12	
12	9	

3

10	12	
12	2	

4

12	7	
8	12	

5

12	1	
4	12	

6

11	12	
12	3	

Practice, Practice, Practice! Multiplication & Division Scholastic Teaching Resources

29

Name _____ Date _____

Busy Kids

For each word problem, follow the directions and complete the sentence. Then write an equation that shows how to multiply to find the product.

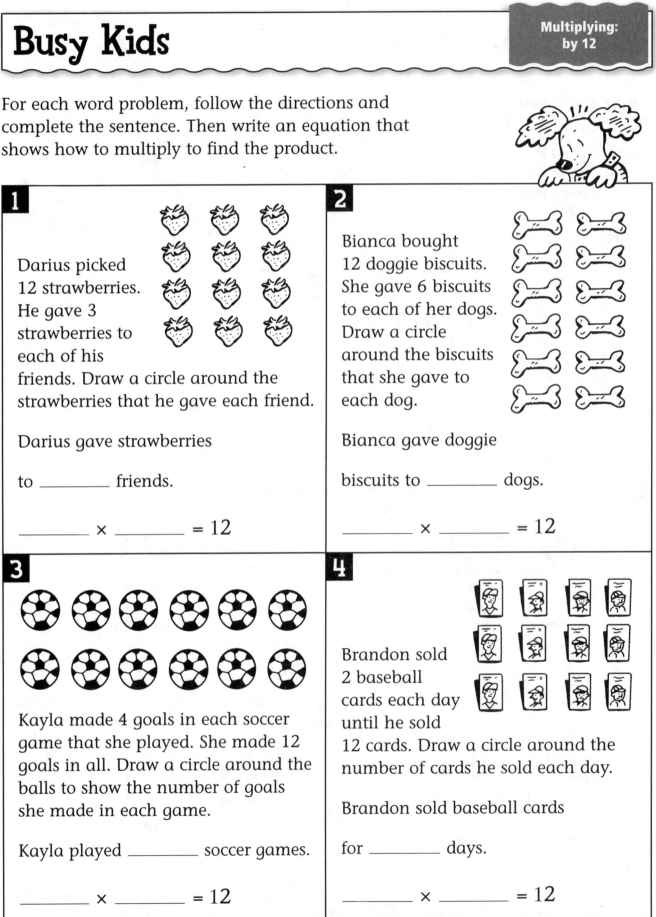

1

Darius picked 12 strawberries. He gave 3 strawberries to each of his friends. Draw a circle around the strawberries that he gave each friend.

Darius gave strawberries

to _____ friends.

_____ × _____ = 12

2

Bianca bought 12 doggie biscuits. She gave 6 biscuits to each of her dogs. Draw a circle around the biscuits that she gave to each dog.

Bianca gave doggie

biscuits to _____ dogs.

_____ × _____ = 12

3

Kayla made 4 goals in each soccer game that she played. She made 12 goals in all. Draw a circle around the balls to show the number of goals she made in each game.

Kayla played _____ soccer games.

_____ × _____ = 12

4

Brandon sold 2 baseball cards each day until he sold 12 cards. Draw a circle around the number of cards he sold each day.

Brandon sold baseball cards

for _____ days.

_____ × _____ = 12

Practice, Practice, Practice! Multiplication & Division Scholastic Teaching Resources

Multiplication Links

Solve the equation in the first link. Write that product in the box in the next link. Then solve the equation in that link. On the back of the page, show how you got your answers.

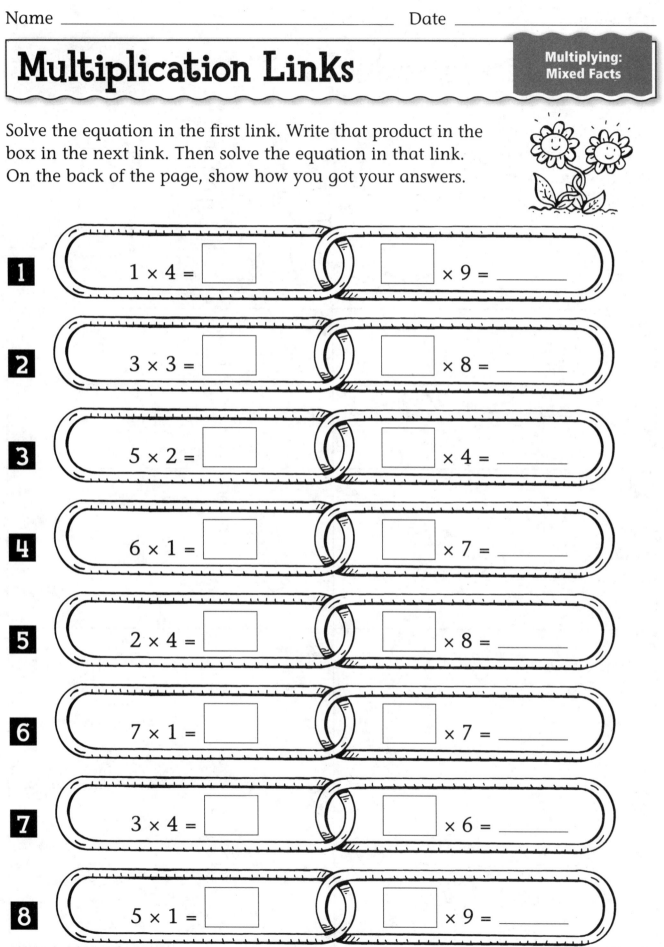

1 $1 \times 4 = \boxed{}$ $\boxed{} \times 9 = \underline{}$

2 $3 \times 3 = \boxed{}$ $\boxed{} \times 8 = \underline{}$

3 $5 \times 2 = \boxed{}$ $\boxed{} \times 4 = \underline{}$

4 $6 \times 1 = \boxed{}$ $\boxed{} \times 7 = \underline{}$

5 $2 \times 4 = \boxed{}$ $\boxed{} \times 8 = \underline{}$

6 $7 \times 1 = \boxed{}$ $\boxed{} \times 7 = \underline{}$

7 $3 \times 4 = \boxed{}$ $\boxed{} \times 6 = \underline{}$

8 $5 \times 1 = \boxed{}$ $\boxed{} \times 9 = \underline{}$

Comparing Products

Solve each equation. Then write
< (is less than), > (is greater than),
or = (is equal to) in the box. The
first one has been done for you.

1

$$\begin{array}{cc} 6 & 3 \\ \times\ 5 & \times 10 \\ \hline 30 & \boxed{=} & 30 \end{array}$$

2

$$\begin{array}{cc} 5 & 8 \\ \times\ 5 & \times\ 3 \end{array}$$

3

$$\begin{array}{cc} 7 & 11 \\ \times\ 9 & \times\ 6 \end{array}$$

4

$$\begin{array}{cc} 2 & 6 \\ \times\ 9 & \times\ 3 \end{array}$$

5

$$\begin{array}{cc} 6 & 5 \\ \times\ 7 & \times\ 8 \end{array}$$

6

$$\begin{array}{cc} 7 & 4 \\ \times\ 2 & \times\ 4 \end{array}$$

7

$$\begin{array}{cc} 7 & 6 \\ \times\ 5 & \times\ 6 \end{array}$$

8

$$\begin{array}{cc} 12 & 9 \\ \times\ 7 & \times\ 9 \end{array}$$

Multiplication Jungle

Solve the problems. Then find your answers in the key to see how to color the picture. Fill in the other spaces with colors of your choice.

Color Key

Answers between	Color
1 and 9	yellow
10 and 20	green
21 and 35	blue
36 and 45	red
46 and 55	brown
56 and 70	purple
71 and 84	orange
85 and 100	pink
101 and 144	white

3×7

11×12

12×12

10×11

7×7

4×5

8×4

6×3

6×6

10×10

9×2

5×8

8×12

8×7

11×6

6×5

8×6

9×8

7×6

9×3

9×11

12×9

1×9

8×8

5×5

8×10

9×6

2×4

5×10

3×3

9×9

3×2

4×9

5×11

7×12

8×2

5×3

Practice, Practice, Practice! Multiplication & Division Scholastic Teaching Resources

33

One by One

Solve each problem. Find the number word in the key for each quotient. Then write the word in the puzzle.

Across

1. $6 \div 1 =$ _____

2. $5 \div 1 =$ _____

3. $12 \div 1 =$ _____

6. $9 \div 1 =$ _____

8. $1 \div 1 =$ _____

9. $4 \div 1 =$ _____

10. $8 \div 1 =$ _____

11. $10 \div 1 =$ _____

Down

1. $7 \div 1 =$ _____

3. $2 \div 1 =$ _____

4. $11 \div 1 =$ _____

5. $0 \div 1 =$ _____

7. $3 \div 1 =$ _____

KEY

zero	seven
one	eight
two	nine
three	ten
four	eleven
five	twelve
six	

Practice, Practice, Practice! Multiplication & Division Scholastic Teaching Resources

Under the Sea

Solve the problems. Then find your quotients in the key to see how to color the picture. Fill in the other spaces with colors of your choice.

Color Key

Quotients	Color
1 or 2	blue
3 or 4	green
5 or 6	purple
7 or 8	red
9 or 10	orange
11 or 12	yellow

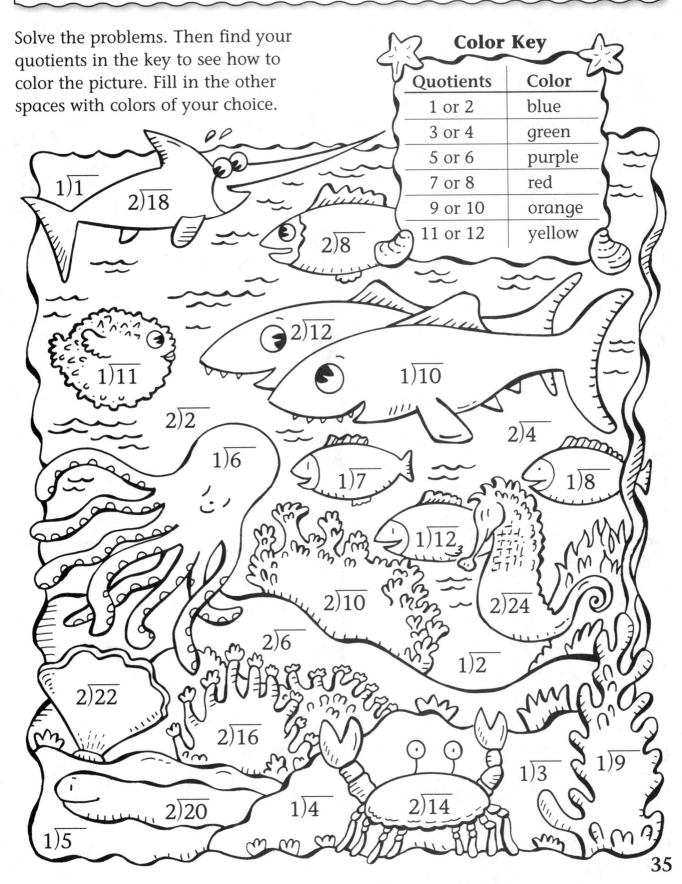

Name _____ Date _____

Crack the Code

Look at the secret symbol in each problem. Check the key to find the symbol and its matching number. Write that number in the equation. Then solve the equation. Use the back of the page to show how you got your answers.

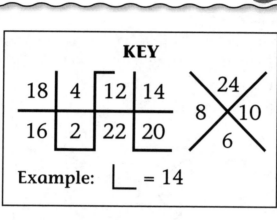

KEY

18	4	12	14
16	2	22	20

24 8 10 6

Example: ⌐ = 14

1
⌐ ÷ 2

_____ ÷ 2 = _____

2
< ÷ 2

_____ ÷ 2 = _____

3
□ ÷ 2

_____ ÷ 2 = _____

4
∟ ÷ 2

_____ ÷ 2 = _____

5
∨ ÷ 2

_____ ÷ 2 = _____

6
⊔ ÷ 2

_____ ÷ 2 = _____

7
⊓ ÷ 2

_____ ÷ 2 = _____

8
> ÷ 2

_____ ÷ 2 = _____

9
∧ ÷ 2

_____ ÷ 2 = _____

10
⊔ ÷ 2

_____ ÷ 2 = _____

11
⊏ ÷ 2

_____ ÷ 2 = _____

12
⌐ ÷ 2

_____ ÷ 2 = _____

36

Solve-and-Seek

Solve the problems. On the back of the page, show how you got your answers. Then find and circle the word for each answer. Hint: Words can go across, down, or diagonally.

1 $24 \div 2 =$ _____

2 $12 \div 2 =$ _____

3 $8 \div 2 =$ _____

4 _____ $\div 2 = 5$

5 $2 \div 2 =$ _____

6 _____ $\div 2 = 8$

7 _____ $\div 2 = 10$

8 $4 \div 2 =$ _____

9 $6 \div 2 =$ _____

10 $14 \div 2 =$ _____

11 _____ $\div 2 = 9$

12 $22 \div 2 =$ _____

```
O S I X T E E N I E B N
F X R A W O T U M P E O
O Q B U E L H Y X N I C
U A F I L O T W O R G A
R W A Y V N S T N S H G
F I P T E N P E P A T R
O H R W U C V I V S E E
V O T A N E T H R E E I
Z C W X L H S J I L N L
U F R E I X R H T S I X
```

Practice, Practice, Practice! Multiplication & Division   Scholastic Teaching Resources

37

Tangled Tennis Shoes

Find the quotients. Use a different color crayon to trace the shoelace that connects each pair of shoes. Then color the shoe in each pair that has the higher quotient.

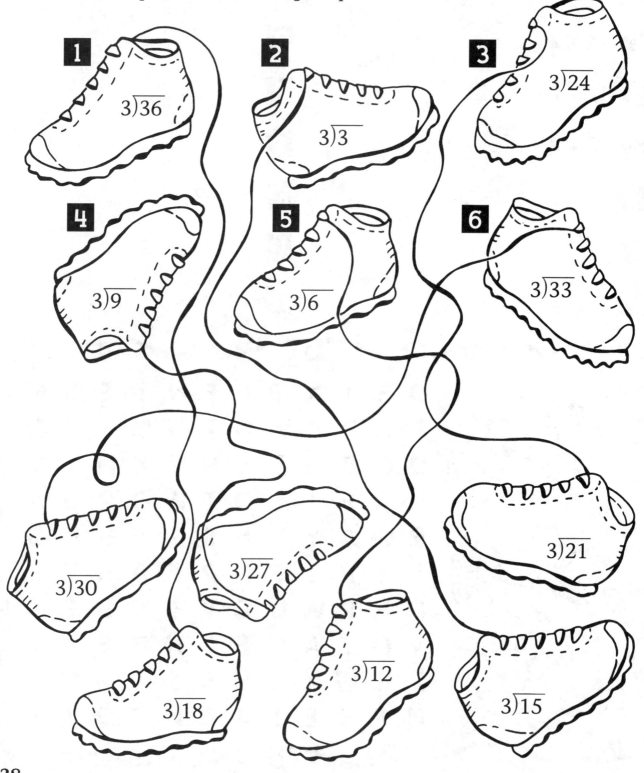

1 $3\overline{)36}$

2 $3\overline{)3}$

3 $3\overline{)24}$

4 $3\overline{)9}$

5 $3\overline{)6}$

6 $3\overline{)33}$

$3\overline{)30}$

$3\overline{)27}$

$3\overline{)21}$

$3\overline{)18}$

$3\overline{)12}$

$3\overline{)15}$

Practice, Practice, Practice! Multiplication & Division Scholastic Teaching Resources

Equations With Three

Find three numbers in a row that can be used to make a correct division equation. Circle the three numbers. You can circle numbers that go across or down. Then write the equation below. The first one has been done for you. Hint: A number can be used more than once.

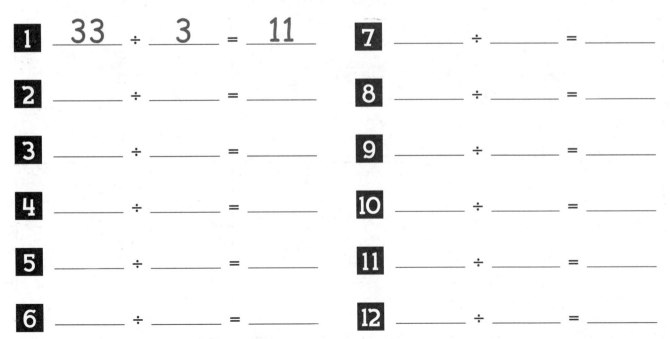

33	4	24	15	6	12
3	30	3	10	3	18
11	15	8	33	2	3
36	3	27	3	9	6
3	5	8	3	3	1
12	3	4	21	3	7

1 _33_ ÷ _3_ = _11_

2 _____ ÷ _____ = _____

3 _____ ÷ _____ = _____

4 _____ ÷ _____ = _____

5 _____ ÷ _____ = _____

6 _____ ÷ _____ = _____

7 _____ ÷ _____ = _____

8 _____ ÷ _____ = _____

9 _____ ÷ _____ = _____

10 _____ ÷ _____ = _____

11 _____ ÷ _____ = _____

12 _____ ÷ _____ = _____

Name _____ Date _____

Flip for Fours

Invite a friend to play this game with you. To play, flip a coin onto a box below. Divide the number in that box by 4 and then write the equation on a sheet of paper. After 12 turns, each player adds the quotients on his or her paper. The player with the higher score wins!

44	40	12
8	28	20
24	48	4
32	36	16

Practice, Practice, Practice! Multiplication & Division Scholastic Teaching Resources

Sea Shopping

Help Donna Dolphin find her way to the Sea Shop. First solve each problem. To show Donna the path, color each piece of coral that has a quotient of 6 or less blue.

Color each piece of coral that has a quotient of 7 or more yellow. Then unscramble the yellow letters to solve the rhyming riddle.

S $4\overline{)32}$

I $4\overline{)16}$

N $4\overline{)12}$

U $4\overline{)16}$

K $4\overline{)12}$

G $4\overline{)20}$

E $4\overline{)28}$

L $4\overline{)48}$

L $4\overline{)40}$

W $4\overline{)40}$

M $4\overline{)24}$

R $4\overline{)8}$

A $4\overline{)32}$

E $4\overline{)36}$

T $4\overline{)24}$

O $4\overline{)16}$

A $4\overline{)36}$

H $4\overline{)44}$

Riddle: What do you call a bargain for a sea mammal?

Answer: A ___ ___ ___ ___ ___ OF A ___ ___ ___ ___!

Name _____ Date _____

Solve It!

For each word problem, write an equation and find the quotient.
On the back of the page, show how you got your answers.

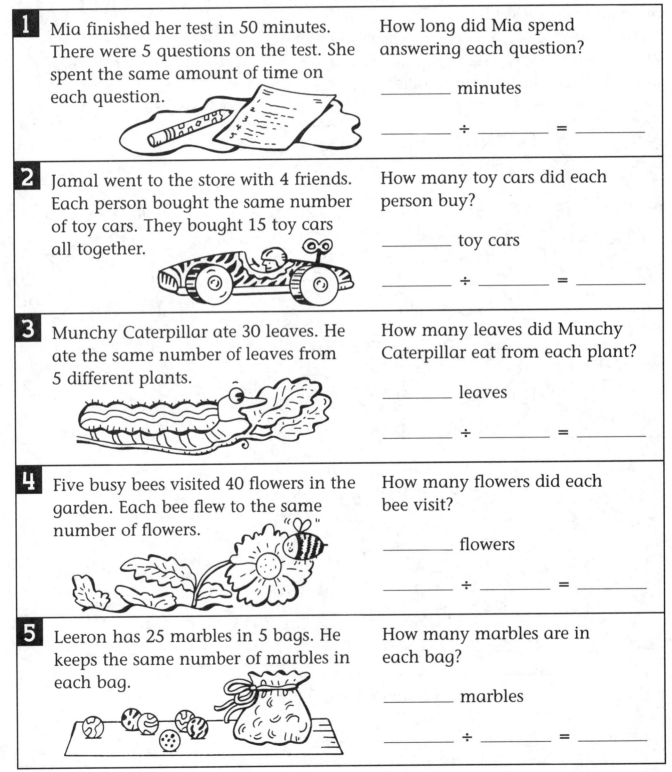

1 Mia finished her test in 50 minutes. There were 5 questions on the test. She spent the same amount of time on each question.

How long did Mia spend answering each question?

_____ minutes

_____ ÷ _____ = _____

2 Jamal went to the store with 4 friends. Each person bought the same number of toy cars. They bought 15 toy cars all together.

How many toy cars did each person buy?

_____ toy cars

_____ ÷ _____ = _____

3 Munchy Caterpillar ate 30 leaves. He ate the same number of leaves from 5 different plants.

How many leaves did Munchy Caterpillar eat from each plant?

_____ leaves

_____ ÷ _____ = _____

4 Five busy bees visited 40 flowers in the garden. Each bee flew to the same number of flowers.

How many flowers did each bee visit?

_____ flowers

_____ ÷ _____ = _____

5 Leeron has 25 marbles in 5 bags. He keeps the same number of marbles in each bag.

How many marbles are in each bag?

_____ marbles

_____ ÷ _____ = _____

Dinosaur Dance

Which dinosaur team won the Jurassic Jitterbug Contest? To find out, solve each equation. Then color each music note that has a matching quotient. The number of the winning team is on the note that you do not color. Write that number on the dinosaur.

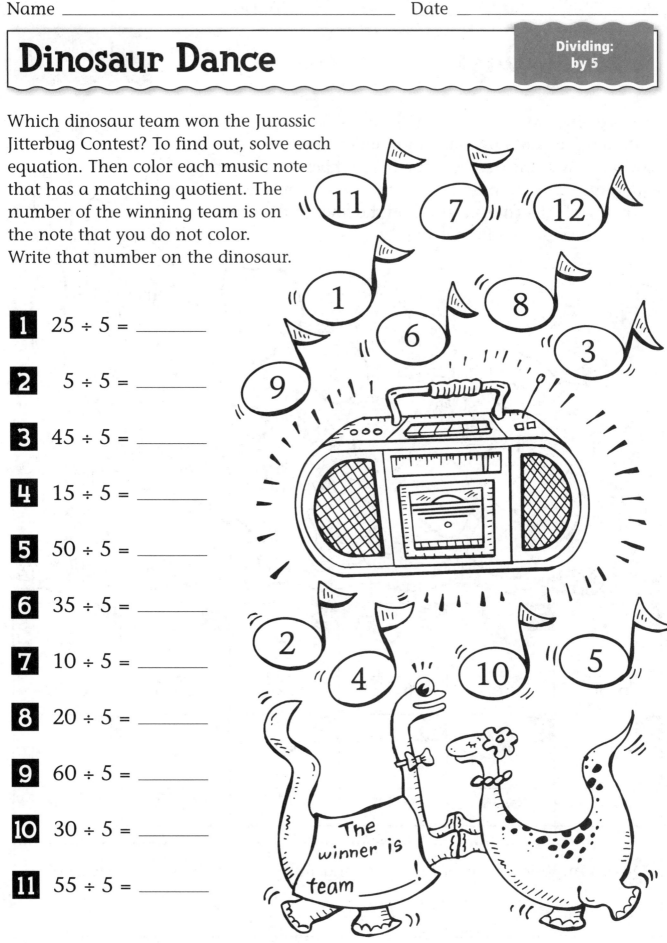

1 25 ÷ 5 = _____

2   5 ÷ 5 = _____

3 45 ÷ 5 = _____

4 15 ÷ 5 = _____

5 50 ÷ 5 = _____

6 35 ÷ 5 = _____

7 10 ÷ 5 = _____

8 20 ÷ 5 = _____

9 60 ÷ 5 = _____

10 30 ÷ 5 = _____

11 55 ÷ 5 = _____

Desert Days

Help Calvin Coyote get to the tall cactus. First, complete the pattern on the path by filling in numbers that are multiples of 6. To answer the question, use the numbers to solve the equations. Color all the boxes that have quotients less than 9. Then write the colored letters on the lines in the same order as they appear in the boxes.

1 S $6\overline{)36}$	**2** A $6\overline{)60}$	**3** C $6\overline{)12}$	**4** O $6\overline{)24}$	**5** T $6\overline{)66}$	**6** R $6\overline{)30}$
7 P $6\overline{)6}$	**8** W $6\overline{)54}$	**9** I $6\overline{)18}$	**10** O $6\overline{)42}$	**11** E $6\overline{)72}$	**12** N $6\overline{)48}$

Question: What is one of the most dangerous desert animals in the world?

Answer: A ___ ___ ___ ___ ___ ___ ___!

Cross Out

Find the two numbers in each box that can be used to complete the equation. Write the numbers in the equation. Then cross out the numbers that you do not use. On the back of the page, show how you got your answers.

1

6   36   7   18

_____ ÷ 6 = _____

2

9   48   36   8

_____ ÷ 6 = _____

3

8   12   2   16

_____ ÷ 6 = _____

4

60   15   6   10

_____ ÷ 6 = _____

5

28   2   24   4

_____ ÷ 6 = _____

6

5   24   30   7

_____ ÷ 6 = _____

7

66   60   11   8

_____ ÷ 6 = _____

8

9   54   60   12

_____ ÷ 6 = _____

9

6   12   1   3

_____ ÷ 6 = _____

10

36   12   72   10

_____ ÷ 6 = _____

11

3   16   30   18

_____ ÷ 6 = _____

12

21   4   42   7

_____ ÷ 6 = _____

Practice, Practice, Practice! Multiplication & Division   Scholastic Teaching Resources

45

Balloon Mix-Up

Find the quotients. Use a different color crayon to trace the string that connects each pair of balloons. Then color the balloon in each pair that has the lower quotient.

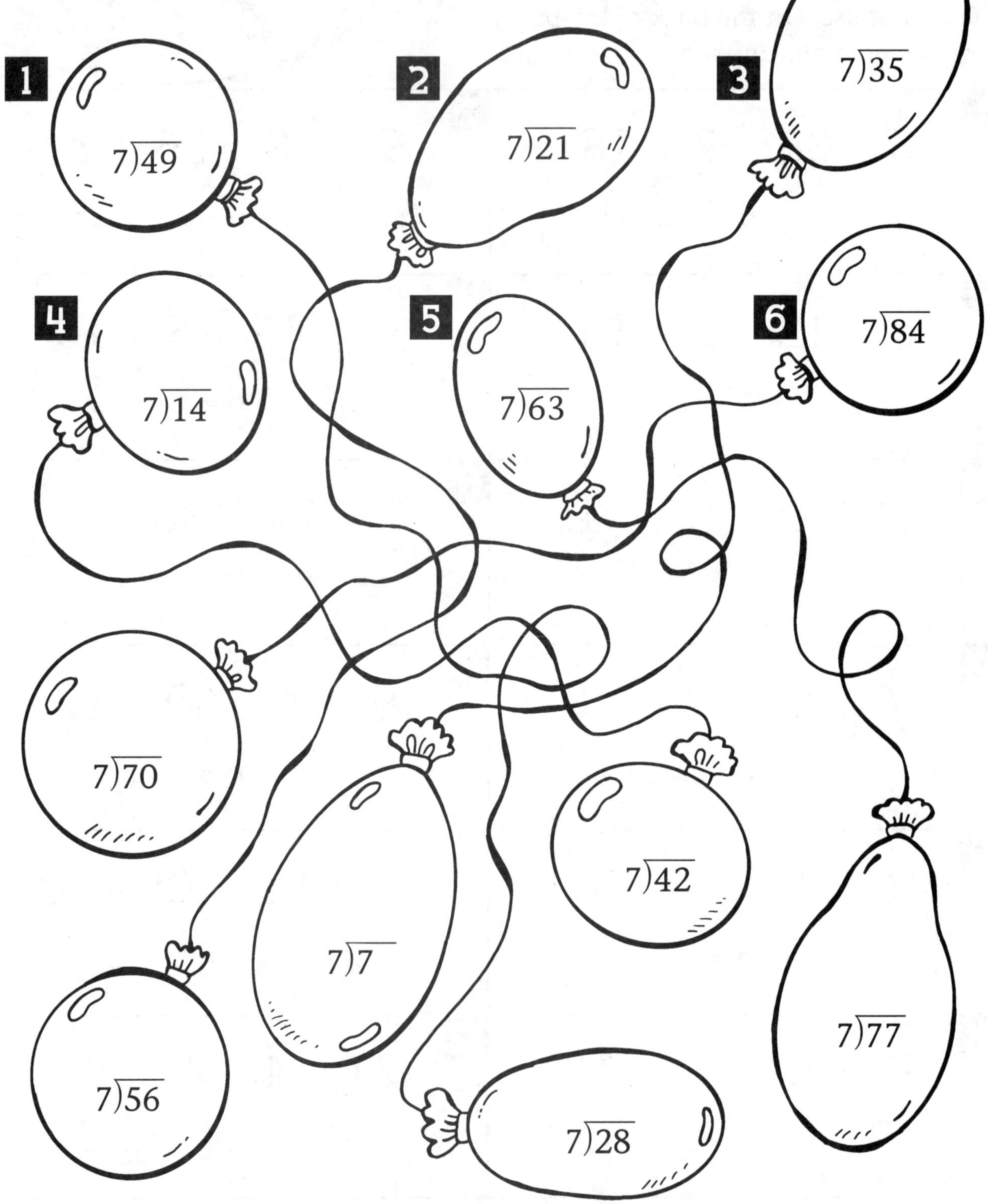

1 $7\overline{)49}$

2 $7\overline{)21}$

3 $7\overline{)35}$

4 $7\overline{)14}$

5 $7\overline{)63}$

6 $7\overline{)84}$

$7\overline{)70}$

$7\overline{)7}$

$7\overline{)42}$

$7\overline{)77}$

$7\overline{)56}$

$7\overline{)28}$

Flower Fun

Dividing: by 7

Find the two petals on each flower that have numbers that can be used to complete the equation. Color those petals and write the numbers in the equation. On the back of the page, show how you got your answers. Hint: The number in the center of each flower is the quotient.

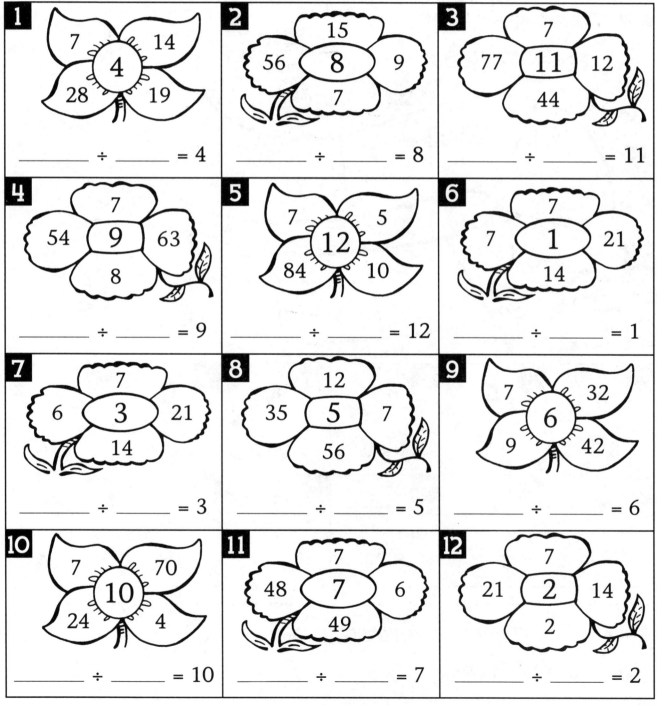

1
7 14 **4** 28 19

_____ ÷ _____ = 4

2
15 56 **8** 9 7

_____ ÷ _____ = 8

3
7 77 **11** 12 44

_____ ÷ _____ = 11

4
7 54 **9** 63 8

_____ ÷ _____ = 9

5
7 5 **12** 84 10

_____ ÷ _____ = 12

6
7 7 **1** 21 14

_____ ÷ _____ = 1

7
7 6 **3** 21 14

_____ ÷ _____ = 3

8
12 35 **5** 7 56

_____ ÷ _____ = 5

9
7 32 **6** 9 42

_____ ÷ _____ = 6

10
7 70 **10** 24 4

_____ ÷ _____ = 10

11
7 48 **7** 6 49

_____ ÷ _____ = 7

12
7 21 **2** 14 2

_____ ÷ _____ = 2

Name _____ Date _____

Sidewalk Stroll

Dottie Dalmatian is ready to take her daily stroll. To complete the number pattern on the sidewalk, fill in the missing numbers that are multiples of 8. To answer the question, use the numbers to solve the equations. Color all the boxes that have quotients higher than 7. Then write the colored letters on the lines in the same order that they appear in the boxes.

8

24

64

88

1 B $8\overline{)32}$	**2** A $8\overline{)8}$	**3** R $8\overline{)80}$	**4** W $8\overline{)40}$	**5** O $8\overline{)96}$	**6** T $8\overline{)16}$
7 E $8\overline{)56}$	**8** L $8\overline{)72}$	**9** H $8\overline{)24}$	**10** I $8\overline{)48}$	**11** L $8\overline{)88}$	**12** S $8\overline{)64}$

Riddle: Why did the hot dog quit acting?

Answer: There weren't any good ___ ___ ___ ___ ___ .

Practice, Practice, Practice! Multiplication & Division Scholastic Teaching Resources

Name _____   Date _____

Divide It Up

For each word problem, write an equation and find the quotient.
On the back of the page, show how you got your answers.

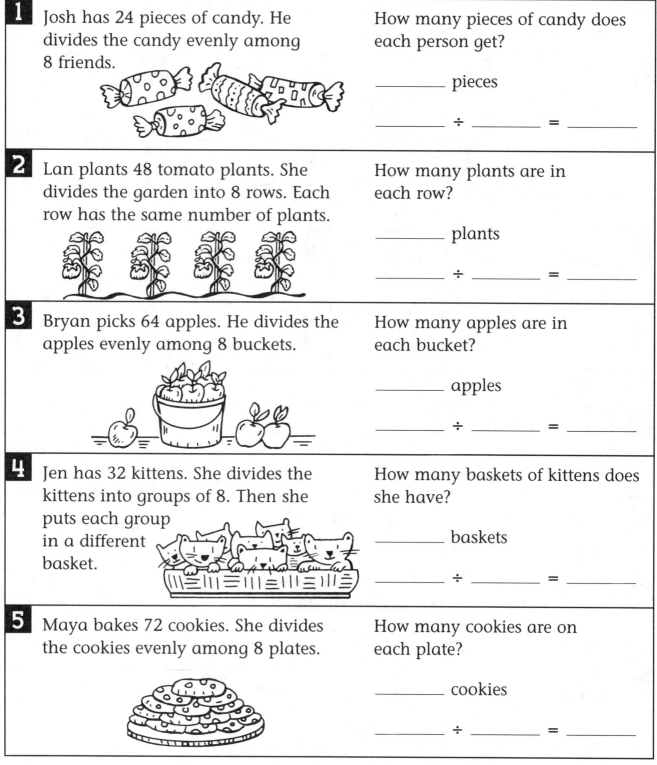

1 Josh has 24 pieces of candy. He divides the candy evenly among 8 friends.

How many pieces of candy does each person get?

_____ pieces

_____ ÷ _____ = _____

2 Lan plants 48 tomato plants. She divides the garden into 8 rows. Each row has the same number of plants.

How many plants are in each row?

_____ plants

_____ ÷ _____ = _____

3 Bryan picks 64 apples. He divides the apples evenly among 8 buckets.

How many apples are in each bucket?

_____ apples

_____ ÷ _____ = _____

4 Jen has 32 kittens. She divides the kittens into groups of 8. Then she puts each group in a different basket.

How many baskets of kittens does she have?

_____ baskets

_____ ÷ _____ = _____

5 Maya bakes 72 cookies. She divides the cookies evenly among 8 plates.

How many cookies are on each plate?

_____ cookies

_____ ÷ _____ = _____

A Trip to the Mall

Solve each problem. Write the quotient on the price tag to show how much each item costs. To find out how much each person spent at the mall, use the price of the items to solve the word problems. In the space under the problem, show how you got your answers. Then write your answer on the line.

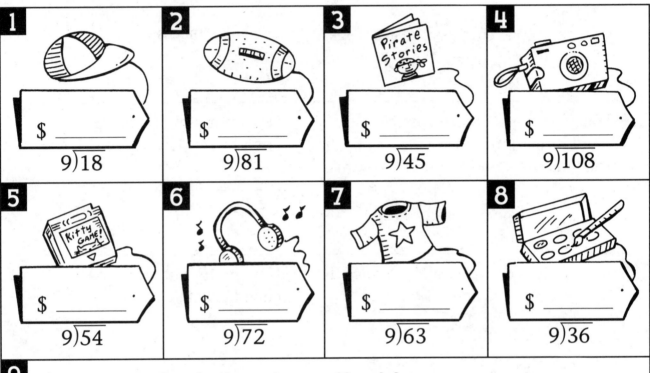

1 $ _____ 9)18

2 $ _____ 9)81

3 $ _____ 9)45

4 $ _____ 9)108

5 $ _____ 9)54

6 $ _____ 9)72

7 $ _____ 9)63

8 $ _____ 9)36

9 Haley bought three books and a set of headphones.

She spent $_____.

10 Manuel bought two caps and a paint set.

He spent $_____.

11 Morgan bought a camera and two footballs.

She spent $_____.

12 Jared bought a video game and two T-shirts.

He spent $_____.

Practice, Practice, Practice! Multiplication & Division Scholastic Teaching Resources

Name _____ Date _____

School Supplies

Look at the chart to find out how many of each school item Ms. Lopez has for her class. Then help her divide the items evenly among her 9 students. Write an equation to show how you got your answer. Then write your answer on the line. The first one has been done for you.

Ms. Lopez's School Supplies

	54 pencils
Glue	18 glue sticks
	27 erasers
	9 pairs of scissors
	108 crayons
	90 sheets of paper
	72 colored markers
	99 paper clips

1 Each student will get

___6___ pencils.

$54 \div 9 = 6$

2 Each student will get

_____ glue sticks.

3 Each student will get

_____ erasers.

4 Each student will get

_____ pair of scissors.

5 Each student will get

_____ crayons.

6 Each student will get

_____ sheets of paper.

7 Each student will get

_____ colored markers.

8 Each student will get

_____ paper clips.

Name _____ Date _____

The Produce Stand

Read each word problem on the chart. Use information from the produce stand to solve the problem. Then write an equation and your answer. The first one has been done for you.

	Word Problem	Equation	Answer
1	Maria paid 50¢ for carrots. How many pounds of carrots did she buy?	$10\overline{)50}^{5}$	___5___ pounds
2	Tim spent 20¢ on cherries. How many pounds of cherries did he buy?	$\overline{)}$	_____ pounds
3	Tonya spent 40¢ on onions. How many pounds of onions did she buy?	$\overline{)}$	_____ pounds
4	Carlos paid 30¢ for apples and grapes. How many pounds of fruit did he buy?	$\overline{)}$	_____ pounds
5	April spent 90¢ on bananas. How many pounds of bananas did she buy?	$\overline{)}$	_____ pounds
6	Joe paid 70¢ for lettuce. How many pounds of lettuce did he buy?	$\overline{)}$	_____ pounds

52

Apple Match

Dividing:
by 10

To help Apple Annie find the matching apple halves, solve the problem in each apple. Then draw a line to the apple half that has the matching quotient. On the back of the page, show how you got your answers.

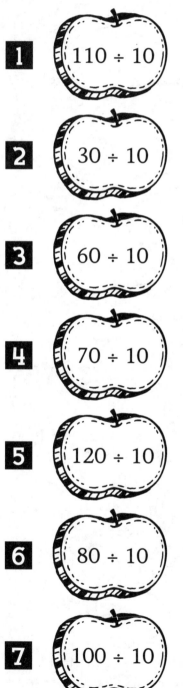

1 $110 \div 10$

2 $30 \div 10$

3 $60 \div 10$

4 $70 \div 10$

5 $120 \div 10$

6 $80 \div 10$

7 $100 \div 10$

6

10

11

3

7

12

8

Lily-Pad Pond

Invite a friend to play this game with you. To play, toss a
penny onto a lily pad. Divide the number on that lily pad
by 11 and then write the equation on a sheet of paper.
After 12 turns, each player adds the quotients on his or
her paper. The player with the higher score wins!

Practice, Practice, Practice! Multiplication & Division Scholastic Teaching Resources

Name _____ Date _____

Around the Track

Solve the equations. Then color the spaces on the race track that have quotients that are greater than 6. To solve the riddle, write the colored letters in on the lines in the same order as they appear on the track.

Start →

Hint: Start at the arrow.

Riddle: Why did the cabbage win the race?

Answer: Because ___ ___ ___ ___ ___ ___ ___ ___ ___ ___ ___ ___ ___ ___ ___!

Practice, Practice, Practice! Multiplication & Division Scholastic Teaching Resources

55

Hidden Treasure

What is the hidden treasure inside the pyramid? To help the explorer find out, solve the equations. Then color all the blocks that have quotients that are less than 7. Unscramble the colored letters. Then write the word on the lines to complete the sentence.

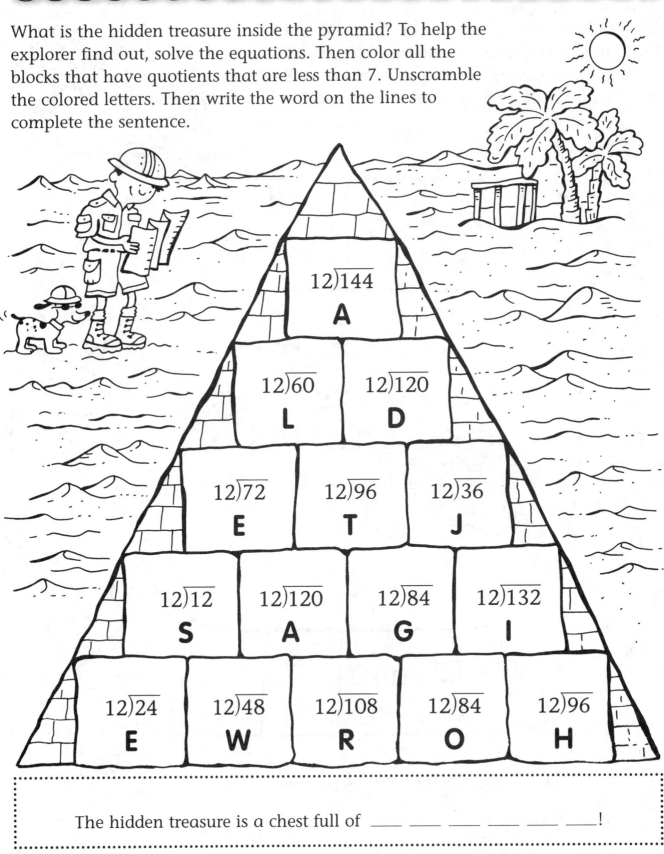

The hidden treasure is a chest full of ___ ___ ___ ___ ___ ___ !

Mystery Letter

Solve the problems. On the back of the page, show how you got your answers. To discover the mystery letter, color all the squares that have quotients of 8 or higher. Write the letter on the line to complete the sentence.

The mystery letter is _____!

1	2	3	4	5
$11\overline{)132}$	$5\overline{)25}$	$8\overline{)48}$	$3\overline{)21}$	$10\overline{)100}$
6 $7\overline{)49}$	**7** $7\overline{)63}$	**8** $12\overline{)36}$	**9** $5\overline{)40}$	**10** $4\overline{)28}$
11 $8\overline{)24}$	**12** $5\overline{)20}$	**13** $9\overline{)81}$	**14** $8\overline{)56}$	**15** $6\overline{)18}$
16 $4\overline{)16}$	**17** $7\overline{)77}$	**18** $3\overline{)15}$	**19** $2\overline{)22}$	**20** $12\overline{)60}$
21 $9\overline{)72}$	**22** $4\overline{)12}$	**23** $6\overline{)36}$	**24** $10\overline{)40}$	**25** $12\overline{)96}$

Practice, Practice, Practice! Multiplication & Division   Scholastic Teaching Resources

57

The Equation Express

Dividing:
Mixed Facts

Read each word problem. Then write an equation and find the quotient. In the space under each problem, show how you got your answer.

1 On the way to Digit Valley, the Equation Express pulled 5 cars. There were 30 people on the train. How many people were in each car?

_____ people

_____ ÷ _____ = _____

2 There were 27 people on the Equation Express when it arrived in Number Valley. The train had 9 cars. How many people were in each car?

_____ people

_____ ÷ _____ = _____

3 The Equation Express carried 63 people in 9 cars on its way to Solution City. How many people were in each car?

_____ people

_____ ÷ _____ = _____

4 On the way to Quotient Hills, the Equation Express pulled 4 cars. There were 32 people on the train. How many people were in each car?

_____ people

_____ ÷ _____ = _____

5 The Equation Express took 49 people to Math Mountain. The train had 7 cars. How many people were in each car?

_____ people

_____ ÷ _____ = _____

Practice, Practice, Practice! Multiplication & Division Scholastic Teaching Resources

Tower Power

Dividing: Mixed Facts

Look at the quotient at the top of each block tower. Then solve the problems on the tower. Color each block that shows a problem that can be answered correctly with the quotient. On the back of the page, show how you got your answers.

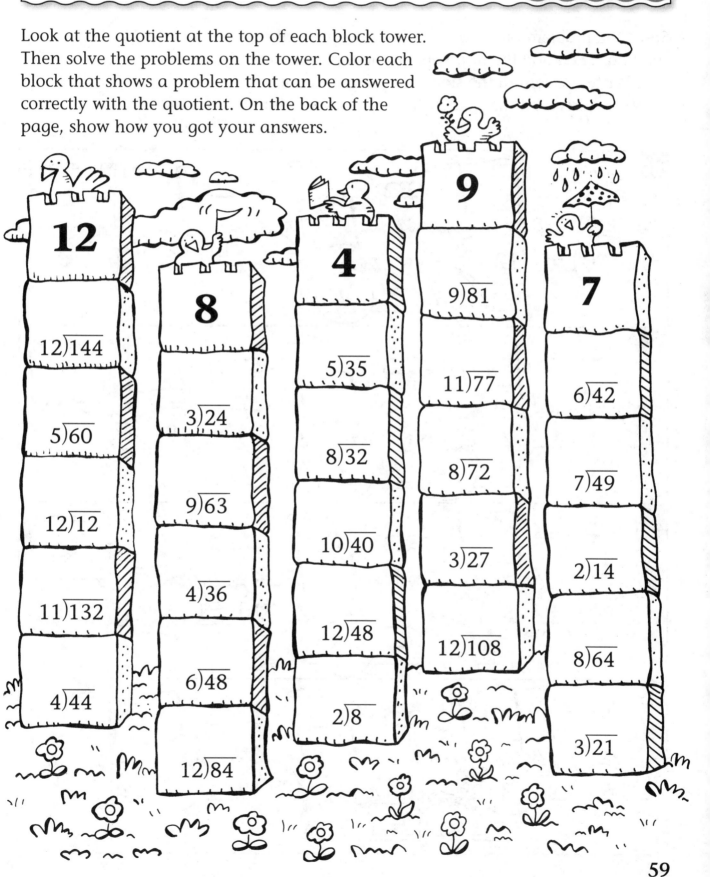

12
$12\overline{)144}$
$5\overline{)60}$
$12\overline{)12}$
$11\overline{)132}$
$4\overline{)44}$

8
$3\overline{)24}$
$9\overline{)63}$
$4\overline{)36}$
$6\overline{)48}$
$12\overline{)84}$

4
$5\overline{)35}$
$8\overline{)32}$
$10\overline{)40}$
$12\overline{)48}$
$2\overline{)8}$

9
$9\overline{)81}$
$11\overline{)77}$
$8\overline{)72}$
$3\overline{)27}$
$12\overline{)108}$

7
$6\overline{)42}$
$7\overline{)49}$
$2\overline{)14}$
$8\overline{)64}$
$3\overline{)21}$

Practice, Practice, Practice! Multiplication & Division Scholastic Teaching Resources

59

Wild Wheels

Solve the problem on each car. Write the quotient on the flag. Then add the numbers on the flags for each row. Write the sum in the sign on the right. If your math is correct, all the signs will have the same sum!

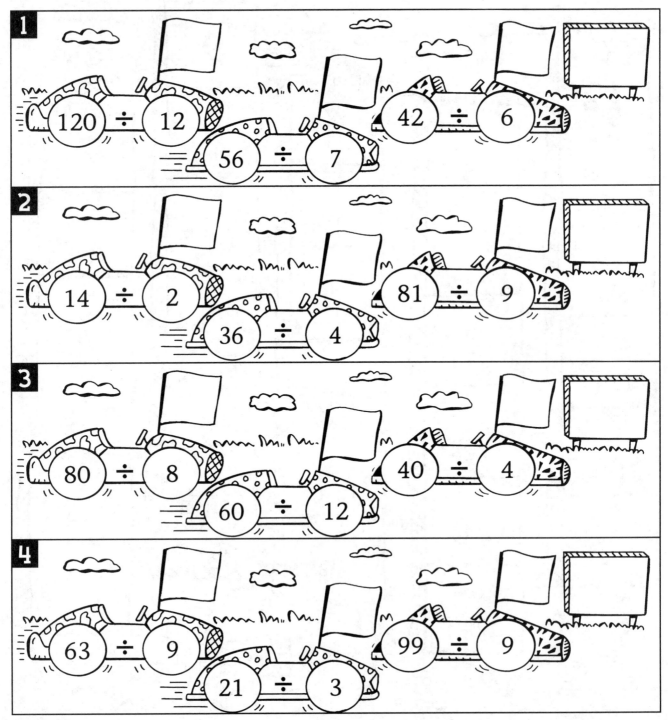

1 $120 \div 12$ $56 \div 7$ $42 \div 6$

2 $14 \div 2$ $36 \div 4$ $81 \div 9$

3 $80 \div 8$ $60 \div 12$ $40 \div 4$

4 $63 \div 9$ $21 \div 3$ $99 \div 9$

Practice, Practice, Practice! Multiplication & Division Scholastic Teaching Resources

Answer Key

Picture Puzzler, page 7

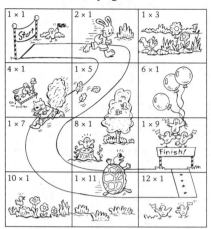

The turtle won the race.

Write the Equation, page 8

1. $7 \times 1 = 7$
2. $2 \times 1 = 2$
3. $10 \times 1 = 10$
4. $8 \times 1 = 8$
5. $6 \times 1 = 6$
6. $12 \times 1 = 12$
7. $9 \times 1 = 9$
8. $5 \times 1 = 5$

Target Practice, page 9

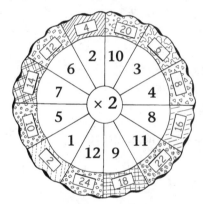

Mountain Climber, page 10

The student should color these numerals to reveal the path: 12, 22, 10, 4, 20, 6, 2, 14, 18, 8, 16, 24.

In the tree: $2 \times 2 = 4$; $2 \times 5 = 10$; $10 \times 2 = 20$; $11 \times 2 = 22$; $2 \times 8 = 16$; $4 \times 2 = 8$; $12 \times 2 = 24$; $6 \times 2 = 12$; $2 \times 7 = 14$; $1 \times 2 = 2$; $2 \times 9 = 18$; $3 \times 2 = 6$

Kitty Riddle, page 11

The student should color the lemons with these numbers: 3, 6, 9, 12, 15, 18, 21, 24, 27, 30, 33, 36

Riddle Answer: I am a sour puss!

At the bottom of the page: $11 \times 3 = 33$; $3 \times 1 = 3$; $3 \times 3 = 9$; $7 \times 3 = 21$; $4 \times 3 = 12$; $3 \times 5 = 15$; $12 \times 3 = 36$; $6 \times 3 = 18$; $3 \times 9 = 27$; $2 \times 3 = 6$; $10 \times 3 = 30$; $8 \times 3 = 24$

Starry Nights, page 12

1. The student should circle 5 rows with 3 stars in each; $5 \times 3 = 15$
2. The student should circle 3 rows with 8 stars in each; $3 \times 8 = 24$
3. The student should circle 3 rows with 6 stars in each; $3 \times 6 = 18$
4. The student should circle 4 rows with 3 stars in each; $4 \times 3 = 12$
5. The student should circle 2 rows with 3 stars in each; $2 \times 3 = 6$
6. The student should circle 3 rows with 10 stars in each; $3 \times 10 = 30$
7. The student should circle 1 row of 3 stars; $1 \times 3 = 3$
8. The student should circle 3 rows with 7 stars in each; $3 \times 7 = 21$

Runaway Riddle, page 13

1. $4 \times 3 = 12$
2. $4 \times 9 = 36$
3. $4 \times 6 = 24$
4. $4 \times 12 = 48$
5. $4 \times 7 = 28$
6. $4 \times 10 = 40$
7. $4 \times 4 = 16$
8. $4 \times 1 = 4$
9. $4 \times 11 = 44$
10. $4 \times 2 = 8$
11. $4 \times 8 = 32$
12. $4 \times 5 = 20$

Riddle Answer: Because seven eight nine!

Crossing Paths, page 14

Path A: 4, 8, 12, 16, 20, 24, 28, 32, 36, 40, 44, 48

Path B: 5, 10, 15, 20, 25, 30, 35, 40, 45, 50, 55

20 and 40 are multiples of 4 and 5. (Note: Students may notice that 60, at the end of path B, is also a multiple of 4 and 5.)

Number Tower, page 15

At the bottom of the page: The mystery product is 55. My equation is $11 \times 5 = 55$.

Lucky Number, page 16

1. $5 \times 5 = 25$
2. $5 \times 12 = 60$
3. $9 \times 5 = 45$
4. $5 \times 1 = 5$
5. $7 \times 5 = 35$
6. $5 \times 11 = 55$
7. $5 \times 3 = 15$
8. $4 \times 5 = 20$
9. $10 \times 5 = 50$
10. $5 \times 0 = 0$
11. $5 \times 6 = 30$
12. $8 \times 5 = 40$

The student should color all the leaves green, except the leaf with 10. The lucky number is 10!

Secret Code, page 17

1. $6 \times 6 = 36$
2. $6 \times 11 = 66$
3. $6 \times 8 = 48$
4. $6 \times 2 = 12$
5. $6 \times 5 = 30$
6. $6 \times 3 = 18$
7. $6 \times 12 = 72$
8. $6 \times 10 = 60$
9. $6 \times 1 = 6$
10. $6 \times 9 = 54$
11. $6 \times 4 = 24$
12. $6 \times 7 = 42$

Hit the Trail!, page 18

1. 4×6 miles $= 24$ miles
2. 3×6 miles $= 18$ miles
3. 7×6 miles $= 42$ miles
4. 9×6 miles $= 54$ miles
5. 2×6 miles $= 12$ miles
6. 6×6 miles $= 36$ miles

Diamond Challenge, page 19

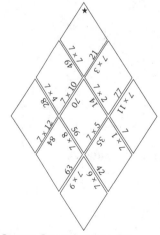

Sunny Sevens, page 20

The student should circle 7, 56, 35, 14, 21, 77, 28, 70, 63, 49, 42, and 84.

$8 \times 7 = 56$; $7 \times 2 = 14$; $12 \times 7 = 84$; $7 \times 1 = 7$; $7 \times 3 = 21$; $5 \times 7 = 35$; $11 \times 7 = 77$; $7 \times 7 = 49$; $9 \times 7 = 63$; $10 \times 7 = 70$; $7 \times 4 = 28$; $6 \times 7 = 42$

Presto Products!, page 21

1. $8 \times 5 = 40$
2. $1 \times 8 = 8$
3. $9 \times 8 = 72$
4. $8 \times 3 = 24$
5. $7 \times 8 = 56$
6. $8 \times 10 = 80$
7. $8 \times 2 = 16$
8. $4 \times 8 = 32$
9. $8 \times 11 = 88$
10. $8 \times 0 = 0$
11. $12 \times 8 = 96$
12. $8 \times 8 = 64$

The magic number is 48!

Easy Eights, page 22

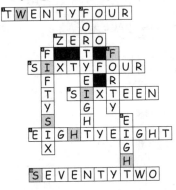

Across

1. $8 \times 3 = 24$
3. $8 \times 0 = 0$
6. $8 \times 8 = 64$
7. $8 \times 2 = 16$
9. $8 \times 11 = 88$
10. $8 \times 9 = 72$

Down

2. $8 \times 6 = 48$
4. $8 \times 7 = 56$
5. $8 \times 5 = 40$
8. $8 \times 1 = 8$

Riddle Answer: A fish wish!

Nine-Square Dare, page 23

On Riley's card, the student should put an X on 90, 63, 27, 36, 72

On Tina's card, the student should put an X on 9, 81, 18, 72, 54, 45, 99

$8 \times 9 = 72$; $9 \times 2 = 18$; $11 \times 9 = 99$; $10 \times 9 = 90$; $9 \times 1 = 9$; $7 \times 9 = 63$; $12 \times 9 = 108$; $9 \times 4 = 36$; $9 \times 9 = 81$; $6 \times 9 = 54$; $3 \times 9 = 27$; $9 \times 5 = 45$

The winner of Nine-Square Dare is Tina.

Prehistoric Pun, page 24

1. $5 \times 9 = 45$
2. $9 \times 9 = 81$
3. $9 \times 12 = 108$
4. $3 \times 9 = 27$
5. $9 \times 2 = 18$
6. $11 \times 9 = 99$
7. $9 \times 7 = 63$
8. $8 \times 9 = 72$
9. $4 \times 9 = 36$
10. $9 \times 6 = 54$
11. $9 \times 10 = 90$

Riddle Answer: A nervous rex!

Lasso Match, page 25

1. 70; The student should draw a line to E.
2. 30; The student should draw a line to F.
3. 40; The student should draw a line to B.
4. 20; The student should draw a line to G.
5. 80; The student should draw a line to A.
6. 50; The student should draw a line to C.
7. 60; The student should draw a line to H.
8. 90; The student should draw a line to D.

Snack Shop, page 26

1. $4 \times 10¢ = 40¢$
2. $8 \times 10¢ = 80¢$
3. $2 \times 10¢ = 20¢$
4. $6 \times 10¢ = 60¢$
5. $1 \times 10¢ = 10¢$
6. $3 \times 10¢ = 30¢$
7. $5 \times 10¢ = 50¢$
8. $9 \times 10¢ = 90¢$
9. $7 \times 10¢ = 70¢$

Teddy Tale, page 27

1. $10 \times 11 = 110$
2. $11 \times 2 = 22$
3. $11 \times 3 = 33$
4. $12 \times 11 = 132$
5. $5 \times 11 = 55$
6. $7 \times 11 = 77$
7. $11 \times 8 = 88$
8. $11 \times 4 = 44$
9. $11 \times 9 = 99$
10. $1 \times 11 = 11$
11. $6 \times 11 = 66$
12. $11 \times 11 = 121$

Riddle Answer: Because they are always stuffed!

Walk the Wall, page 28

$7 \times 11 = 77$; $11 \times 2 = 22$; $8 \times 11 = 88$; $11 \times 1 = 11$; $11 \times 11 = 121$; $10 \times 11 = 110$; $11 \times 3 = 33$; $12 \times 11 = 132$; $4 \times 11 = 44$; $11 \times 6 = 66$; $9 \times 11 = 99$; $11 \times 5 = 55$

The student should color these numbers on the wall: 33, 88, 55, 22, 77, 99, 11, 110, 121, 66, 44, and 132.

Magic Multiplication, page 29

1

12	3	36
5	12	60
60	36	96

2

6	12	72
12	9	108
72	108	180

3

10	12	120
12	2	24
120	24	144

4

12	7	84
8	12	96
96	84	180

5

12	1	12
4	12	48
48	12	60

6

11	12	132
12	3	36
132	36	168

Busy Kids, page 30

1. The student should circle 4 sets of 3 strawberries. Darius gave strawberries to 4 friends. $3 \times 4 = 12$
2. The student should circle 2 sets of 6 doggie biscuits. Bianca gave doggie biscuits to 2 dogs. $6 \times 2 = 12$
3. The student should circle 3 sets of 4 soccer balls. Kayla played 3 soccer games. $4 \times 3 = 12$
4. The student should circle 6 sets of 2 cards. Brandon sold baseball cards for 6 days. $2 \times 6 = 12$

Multiplication Links, page 31

1. $1 \times 4 = 4$; $4 \times 9 = 36$
2. $3 \times 3 = 9$; $9 \times 8 = 72$
3. $5 \times 2 = 10$; $10 \times 4 = 40$
4. $6 \times 1 = 6$; $6 \times 7 = 42$
5. $2 \times 4 = 8$; $8 \times 8 = 64$
6. $7 \times 1 = 7$; $7 \times 7 = 49$
7. $3 \times 4 = 12$; $12 \times 6 = 72$
8. $5 \times 1 = 5$; $5 \times 9 = 45$

Comparing Products, page 32

1. $6 \times 5 = 30$; $3 \times 10 = 30$; $30 = 30$
2. $5 \times 5 = 25$; $8 \times 3 = 24$; $25 > 24$
3. $7 \times 9 = 63$; $11 \times 6 = 66$; $63 < 66$
4. $2 \times 9 = 18$; $6 \times 3 = 18$; $18 = 18$
5. $6 \times 7 = 42$; $5 \times 8 = 40$; $42 > 40$
6. $7 \times 2 = 14$; $4 \times 4 = 16$; $14 < 16$
7. $7 \times 5 = 35$; $6 \times 6 = 36$; $35 < 36$
8. $12 \times 7 = 84$; $9 \times 9 = 81$; $84 > 81$

Multiplication Jungle, page 33

The student should use the following colors to color each space that has a corresponding problem.

yellow: 2×4; 3×2; 1×9; 3×3

green: 4×5; 8×2; 5×3; 9×2; 6×3

blue: 3×7; 8×4; 6×5; 9×3; 5×5

red: 4×9; 6×6; 5×8; 7×6

brown: 7×7; 8×6; 5×11; 9×6; 5×10

purple: 8×7; 8×8; 11×6

orange: 9×8; 8×10; 9×9; 7×12

pink: 8×12; 10×10; 9×11

white: 12×12; 11×12; 10×11; 12×9

One by One, page 34

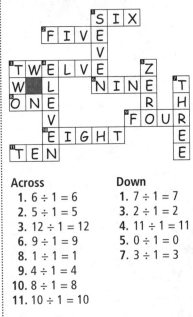

Across

1. $6 \div 1 = 6$
2. $5 \div 1 = 5$
3. $12 \div 1 = 12$
6. $9 \div 1 = 9$
8. $1 \div 1 = 1$
9. $4 \div 1 = 4$
10. $8 \div 1 = 8$
11. $10 \div 1 = 10$

Down

1. $7 \div 1 = 7$
3. $2 \div 1 = 2$
4. $11 \div 1 = 11$
5. $0 \div 1 = 0$
7. $3 \div 1 = 3$

Under the Sea, page 35

The student should use the following colors to color each space that has a corresponding problem.

blue: $1\overline{)1}^{1}$, $1\overline{)2}^{2}$, $2\overline{)2}^{1}$, $2\overline{)4}^{2}$

green: $1\overline{)3}^{3}$, $1\overline{)4}^{4}$, $2\overline{)6}^{3}$, $2\overline{)8}^{4}$

purple: $1\overline{)5}^{5}$, $1\overline{)6}^{6}$, $2\overline{)10}^{5}$, $2\overline{)12}^{6}$

red: $1\overline{)7}^{7}$, $1\overline{)8}^{8}$, $2\overline{)14}^{7}$, $2\overline{)16}^{8}$

orange: $1\overline{)9}^{9}$, $1\overline{)10}^{10}$, $2\overline{)18}^{9}$, $2\overline{)20}^{10}$

yellow: $1\overline{)11}^{11}$, $1\overline{)12}^{12}$, $2\overline{)22}^{11}$, $2\overline{)24}^{12}$

Crack the Code, page 36

1. $18 \div 2 = 9$
2. $10 \div 2 = 5$
3. $2 \div 2 = 1$
4. $14 \div 2 = 7$
5. $24 \div 2 = 12$
6. $12 \div 2 = 6$
7. $22 \div 2 = 11$
8. $8 \div 2 = 4$
9. $6 \div 2 = 3$
10. $4 \div 2 = 2$
11. $20 \div 2 = 10$
12. $16 \div 2 = 8$

Solve-and-Seek, page 37

1. $24 \div 2 = 12$
2. $12 \div 2 = 6$
3. $8 \div 2 = 4$
4. $10 \div 2 = 5$
5. $2 \div 2 = 1$
6. $16 \div 2 = 8$
7. $20 \div 2 = 10$
8. $4 \div 2 = 2$
9. $6 \div 2 = 3$
10. $14 \div 2 = 7$
11. $18 \div 2 = 9$
12. $22 \div 2 = 11$

Tangled Tennis Shoes, page 38

1. $3\overline{)36}^{12}$, $3\overline{)18}^{6}$; The student should color the top shoe in the pair.

2. $3\overline{)3}^{1}$, $3\overline{)15}^{5}$; The student should color the bottom shoe in the pair.

3. $3\overline{)24}^{8}$, $3\overline{)21}^{7}$; The student should color the top shoe in the pair.

4. $3\overline{)9}^{3}$, $3\overline{)27}^{9}$; The student should color the bottom shoe in the pair.

5. $3\overline{)6}^{2}$, $3\overline{)12}^{4}$; The student should color the bottom shoe in the pair.

6. $3\overline{)33}^{11}$, $3\overline{)30}^{10}$; The student should color the top shoe in the pair.

Equations With Three, page 39

Across

$30 \div 3 = 10$
$27 \div 3 = 9$
$3 \div 3 = 1$
$12 \div 3 = 4$
$21 \div 3 = 7$

Down

$33 \div 3 = 11$
$24 \div 3 = 8$
$6 \div 3 = 2$
$18 \div 3 = 6$
$15 \div 3 = 5$
$36 \div 3 = 12$
$9 \div 3 = 3$

33	4	24	15	6	12
3	30	3	10	3	18
11	15	8	33	2	3
36	3	27	3	9	6
3	5	8	3	3	1
12	3	4	21	3	7

The student should write the problems above in any order.

Flip for Fours, page 40

The student should write 12 division equations on a sheet of paper. The sum of the quotients will vary for each player.

Sea Shopping, page 41

Riddle Answer: A whale of a sale!

Solve It!, page 42

1. 10 minutes; $50 \div 5 = 10$
2. 3 toy cars; $15 \div 5 = 3$
3. 6 leaves; $30 \div 5 = 6$
4. 8 flowers; $40 \div 5 = 8$
5. 5 marbles; $25 \div 5 = 5$

Dinosaur Dance, page 43

1. $25 \div 5 = 5$
2. $5 \div 5 = 1$
3. $45 \div 5 = 9$
4. $15 \div 5 = 3$
5. $50 \div 5 = 10$
6. $35 \div 5 = 7$
7. $10 \div 5 = 2$
8. $20 \div 5 = 4$
9. $60 \div 5 = 12$
10. $30 \div 5 = 6$
11. $55 \div 5 = 11$

The winner is team 8!

Desert Days, page 44

The student should complete the path so that it includes the following numbers: 6, 12, 18, 24, 30, 36, 42, 48, 54, 60, 66, 72.

1. 6   2. 10   3. 2   4. 4
5. 11   6. 5   7. 1   8. 9
9. 3   10. 7   11. 12   12. 8

The student should color these boxes: 1., 3., 4., 6., 7., 9., 10., and 12.

Answer: A scorpion!

Cross Out, page 45

1. $36 \div 6 = 6$ 2. $48 \div 6 = 8$
3. $12 \div 6 = 2$ 4. $60 \div 6 = 10$
5. $24 \div 6 = 4$ 6. $30 \div 6 = 5$
7. $66 \div 6 = 11$ 8. $54 \div 6 = 9$
9. $6 \div 6 = 1$ 10. $72 \div 6 = 12$
11. $18 \div 6 = 3$ 12. $42 \div 6 = 7$

Balloon Mix-Up, page 46

1. $7\overline{)49}^{7}$, $7\overline{)28}^{4}$; The student should color the bottom balloon in the pair.

2. $7\overline{)21}^{3}$, $7\overline{)56}^{8}$; The student should color the top balloon in the pair.

3. $7\overline{)35}^{5}$, $7\overline{)7}^{1}$; The student should color the bottom balloon in the pair.

4. $7\overline{)14}^{2}$, $7\overline{)42}^{6}$; The student should color the top balloon in the pair.

5. $7\overline{)63}^{9}$, $7\overline{)77}^{11}$; The student should color the top balloon in the pair.

6. $7\overline{)84}^{12}$, $7\overline{)70}^{10}$; The student should color the bottom balloon in the pair.

Flower Fun, page 47

1. $28 \div 7 = 4$
2. $56 \div 7 = 8$
3. $77 \div 7 = 11$
4. $63 \div 7 = 9$
5. $84 \div 7 = 12$
6. $7 \div 7 = 1$
7. $21 \div 7 = 3$
8. $35 \div 7 = 5$
9. $42 \div 7 = 6$
10. $70 \div 7 = 10$
11. $49 \div 7 = 7$
12. $14 \div 7 = 2$

Sidewalk Stroll, page 48

The student should complete the path so that it includes the following numbers: 8, 16, 24, 32, 40, 48, 56, 64, 72, 80, 88, 96.

1. $8)\overline{32} = 4$
2. $8)\overline{8} = 1$
3. $8)\overline{80} = 10$
4. $8)\overline{40} = 5$
5. $8)\overline{96} = 12$
6. $8)\overline{16} = 2$
7. $8)\overline{56} = 7$
8. $8)\overline{72} = 9$
9. $8)\overline{24} = 3$
10. $8)\overline{48} = 6$
11. $8)\overline{88} = 11$
12. $8)\overline{64} = 8$

The student should color these boxes: 3., 5., 8., 11., and 12.

Riddle Answer: There weren't any good rolls.

Divide It Up, page 49

1. 3 pieces; $24 \div 8 = 3$
2. 6 plants; $48 \div 8 = 6$
3. 8 apples; $64 \div 8 = 8$
4. 4 baskets; $32 \div 8 = 4$
5. 9 cookies; $72 \div 8 = 9$

A Trip to the Mall, page 50

1. $2
2. $9
3. $5
4. $12
5. $6
6. $8
7. $7
8. $4
9. She spent $23.
10. He spent $8.
11. She spent $30.
12. He spent $20.

School Supplies, page 51

1. Each student will get 6 pencils.
2. Each student will get 2 glue sticks.
3. Each student will get 3 erasers.
4. Each student will get 1 pair of scissors.
5. Each student will get 12 crayons.
6. Each student will get 10 sheets of paper.
7. Each student will get 8 colored markers.
8. Each student will get 11 paper clips.

The Produce Stand, page 52

1. $10)\overline{50} = 5$; 5 pounds
2. $10)\overline{20} = 2$; 2 pounds
3. $10)\overline{40} = 4$; 4 pounds
4. $10)\overline{30} = 3$; 3 pounds
5. $10)\overline{90} = 9$; 9 pounds
6. $10)\overline{70} = 7$; 7 pounds

Apple Match, page 53

1. The student should draw a line to the apple with 11.
2. The student should draw a line to the apple with 3.
3. The student should draw a line to the apple with 6.
4. The student draw a line to the apple with 7.
5. The student should draw a line to the apple with 12.
6. The student should draw a line to the apple with 8.
7. The student should draw a line to the apple with 10.

Lily-Pad Pond, page 54

The student should write 12 division equations on a sheet of paper. The sum of the quotients will vary for each player.

Around the Track, page 55

The student should color all the spaces that have quotients greater than 6 (shown here in bold).

$11)\overline{33} = 3$; $12)\overline{120} = \mathbf{10}$; $11)\overline{66} = 6$; $12)\overline{84} = \mathbf{7}$; $12)\overline{48} = 4$;

$11)\overline{11} = 1$; $11)\overline{132} = \mathbf{12}$; $12)\overline{144} = \mathbf{12}$; $11)\overline{55} = 5$; $11)\overline{99} = \mathbf{9}$;

$12)\overline{24} = 2$; $12)\overline{96} = \mathbf{8}$; $11)\overline{44} = 4$; $11)\overline{121} = \mathbf{11}$; $11)\overline{22} = 2$;

$12)\overline{108} = \mathbf{9}$; $12)\overline{60} = 5$; $11)\overline{88} = \mathbf{8}$; $11)\overline{77} = \mathbf{7}$; $12)\overline{72} = 6$

Riddle Answer: Because it was a head!

Hidden Treasure, page 56

The student should color all the blocks on the pyramid that have quotients less than 7 (shown here in bold).

$12)\overline{144} = 12$; $12)\overline{60} = \mathbf{5}$; $12)\overline{120} = 10$; $12)\overline{72} = \mathbf{6}$; $12)\overline{96} = 8$;

$12)\overline{36} = \mathbf{3}$; $12)\overline{12} = \mathbf{1}$; $12)\overline{120} = 10$; $12)\overline{84} = 7$; $12)\overline{132} = 11$;

$12)\overline{24} = \mathbf{2}$; $12)\overline{48} = \mathbf{4}$; $12)\overline{108} = 9$; $12)\overline{84} = 7$; $12)\overline{96} = 8$

The hidden treasure is a chest full of jewels!

Mystery Letter, page 57

The student should color all the squares that have quotients of 8 or more (shown here in bold).

1. $11)\overline{132} = \mathbf{12}$
2. $5)\overline{25} = 5$
3. $8)\overline{48} = 6$
4. $3)\overline{21} = 7$
5. $10)\overline{100} = \mathbf{10}$
6. $7)\overline{49} = 7$
7. $7)\overline{63} = \mathbf{9}$
8. $12)\overline{36} = 3$
9. $5)\overline{40} = \mathbf{8}$
10. $4)\overline{28} = 7$
11. $8)\overline{24} = 3$
12. $5)\overline{20} = 4$
13. $9)\overline{81} = \mathbf{9}$
14. $8)\overline{56} = 7$
15. $6)\overline{18} = 3$
16. $4)\overline{16} = 4$
17. $7)\overline{77} = \mathbf{11}$
18. $3)\overline{15} = 5$
19. $2)\overline{22} = \mathbf{11}$
20. $12)\overline{60} = 5$
21. $9)\overline{72} = \mathbf{8}$
22. $4)\overline{12} = 3$
23. $6)\overline{36} = 6$
24. $10)\overline{40} = 4$
25. $12)\overline{96} = \mathbf{8}$

The mystery letter is X!

The Equation Express, page 58

1. 6 people; $30 \div 5 = 6$
2. 3 people; $27 \div 9 = 3$
3. 7 people; $63 \div 9 = 7$
4. 8 people; $32 \div 4 = 8$
5. 7 people; $49 \div 7 = 7$

Tower Power, page 59

For each tower, the student should color the blocks with the quotients that are shown here in bold.

12: $12)\overline{144} = \mathbf{12}$; $5)\overline{60} = \mathbf{12}$; $12)\overline{12} = 1$; $11)\overline{132} = \mathbf{12}$; $4)\overline{44} = 11$

8: $3)\overline{24} = \mathbf{8}$; $9)\overline{63} = 7$; $4)\overline{36} = 9$; $6)\overline{48} = \mathbf{8}$; $12)\overline{84} = 7$

4: $5)\overline{35} = 7$; $8)\overline{32} = \mathbf{4}$; $10)\overline{40} = \mathbf{4}$; $12)\overline{48} = \mathbf{4}$; $2)\overline{8} = \mathbf{4}$

9: $9)\overline{81} = \mathbf{9}$; $11)\overline{77} = 7$; $8)\overline{72} = \mathbf{9}$; $3)\overline{27} = \mathbf{9}$; $12)\overline{108} = \mathbf{9}$

7: $6)\overline{42} = \mathbf{7}$; $7)\overline{49} = \mathbf{7}$; $2)\overline{14} = \mathbf{7}$; $8)\overline{64} = 8$; $3)\overline{21} = \mathbf{7}$

Wild Wheels, page 60

1. $120 \div 12 = 10$, $56 \div 7 = 8$, $42 \div 6 = 7$; 25
2. $14 \div 2 = 7$, $36 \div 4 = 9$, $81 \div 9 = 9$; 25
3. $80 \div 8 = 10$, $60 \div 12 = 5$, $40 \div 4 = 10$; 25
4. $63 \div 9 = 7$, $21 \div 3 = 7$, $99 \div 9 = 11$; 25